Advances in Mental Health and Addiction

# SpringerBriefs in Advances in Mental Health and Addiction

**Series Editor**

Masood Zangeneh, Humber College, Woodbridge, Ontario, Canada

Over the past several decades we have witnessed dramatic shifts in prevailing approaches to mental health and addiction. Significant scientific achievements have led to novel treatment options that impacted the experiences of individuals with mental disorders. In recent years, new perspectives have begun to influence the way we address mental health and substance dependencies, resulting in a greater emphasis on mental health promotion and prevention strategies. Despite these progressions, mental health care systems too often remain stagnant, fragmented, and peripheral.

This sub-series provides an opportunity to expand upon cutting-edge research being presented at mental health or addiction related conferences or colloquia around the world. Each volume is dedicated to a singular event and provides an opportunity for scholars to present their research and get feedback from other scholars in their field.

Sachin Batra
Editor

# Socioeconomic Factors, Consumer Health, and Broader Well-Being

Springer

*Editor*
Sachin Batra
NICMAR University
Pune, Maharashtra, India

ISSN 2570-3390 ISSN 2570-3404 (electronic)
Advances in Mental Health and Addiction
ISSN 2948-2224 ISSN 2948-2232 (electronic)
SpringerBriefs in Advances in Mental Health and Addiction
ISBN 978-3-032-05633-7 ISBN 978-3-032-05634-4 (eBook)
https://doi.org/10.1007/978-3-032-05634-4



This Springer imprint is published by the registered company Springer Nature Switzerland AG
The registered company address is: Gewerbestrasse 11, 6330 Cham, Switzerland

# Preface

This edited volume, Socioeconomic Factors, Consumer Health, and Broader Well-Being, is the outcome of a vibrant exchange of ideas and research insights presented at the conference on "Health and Wellness for All," held at NICMAR University, Pune, on February 15, 2025. The conference was generously sponsored by the Indian Council of Social Science Research (ICSSR), New Delhi, as part of its Special Call for Vision Viksit Bharat@2047, an initiative aimed at fostering inclusive and sustainable development in India.

The volume brings together interdisciplinary contributions that critically examine the complex intersections between socioeconomic determinants, consumer behavior, and health outcomes. Each chapter reflects a unique lens, ranging from gender and mental health to cultural wellness practices and elderly care, capturing both the diversity of lived experiences and the systemic factors that shape well-being.

In "Bridging Gaps in Adolescent Health and Hygiene Education," we explore community-based interventions among tribal adolescents in Purulia, West Bengal. "Empowering Women Through Workplace Wellness" highlights innovative strategies from Bangladesh aimed at promoting gender-inclusive health environments. The chapter on urban mental health delves into gendered patterns of psychological well-being within rapidly changing cityscapes. In contrast, "Dancing Away Stress" offers a creative and holistic approach to emotional regulation through expressive movement. Lastly, "I Am Alone but Not Lonely" investigates how living arrangements among older Indian adults influence their sense of autonomy and quality of life.

Together, these chapters foreground a critical message: that health and well-being are deeply social phenomena: shaped by culture, context, opportunity, and inequality. In aligning with the Vision Viksit Bharat agenda, this volume emphasizes that achieving holistic national development requires a sustained focus on social inclusion, gender equity, and mental and physical wellness across all stages of life.

We extend our deepest gratitude to the ICSSR for their continued support and vision. The event was supported by NICMAR University's leadership, including Dr. Sushma S. Kulkarni (Vice Chancellor). We especially acknowledge the efforts of the entire organizing committee for bringing this initiative to life. We also thank all the contributors for their scholarly commitment and the peer reviewers for their valuable feedback. It is our hope that this volume not only contributes to academic discourse but also informs future policy and practice toward building a healthier and more equitable India by 2047.

Pune, Maharashtra, India
December 2025

Sachin Batra

# Acknowledgements

We gratefully acknowledge the support of the Indian Council of Social Science Research (ICSSR), New Delhi, India, for sponsoring this initiative under a Special Call for Vision Viksit Bharat @ 2047.

This work was supported by Indian Council of Social Science Research (ICSSR), New Delhi.

# Contents

# Bridging Gaps in Adolescent Health and Hygiene Education: An Analysis of CESR's Efforts in Ayodhya Hill, Purulia

**Abhisek Panda and Laxmiram Gope**

## 1 Introduction

Adolescent health and hygiene education is essential for promoting physical and mental well-being during this transformative stage of life. During this period, young individuals are significantly more curious about the opposite sex and develop feelings and affection for one another. Hence, in this emotionally ebullient stage, we must provide ample opportunity to understand the world, life, and relationships, enabling them to recognize and comprehend the changes that occur during adolescence. Particularly, parents, teachers, and other stakeholders, such as NGOs, play a pivotal role in transforming the perceptions of adolescent children. According to their curiosity, needs, and psychological aspects, we must consider the curriculum design and course content. Adolescents, particularly girls, face unique challenges related to menstruation, personal hygiene, and reproductive health, which can significantly impact their academic performance, self-esteem, and overall development (WHO, 2020). Educating adolescents about these issues is essential for breaking cycles of misinformation and entrenched stereotypes, reducing health risks, thus empowering them to make informed choices. Despite government efforts, many rural and tribal areas still lack effective health education programmes, leaving adolescents vulnerable to preventable health issues (UNICEF, 2019). According to a UNICEF (2020) report, approximately 70% of girls in rural India remain unaware of menstruation until their first period. The ASER report (2022) also identified that only 68% of schools in India have functional girls' toilets. The concerning images

A. Panda (✉) · L. Gope
School of Education, Adamas University, Kolkata, West Bengal, India

Department of Education, Sidho-Kanho-Birsha University, Purulia, West Bengal, India

 
S. Batra (ed.), *Socioeconomic Factors, Consumer Health, and Broader Well-Being*, Advances in Mental Health and Addiction, https://doi.org/10.1007/978-3-032-05634-4_1

presented by the UDISE (2021) report are shocking, revealing that 44% of schools lack access to water for hygiene purposes in toilets.

The situation is more deplorable in rural India, particularly in regions like Ayodhya Hill in the Purulia district of West Bengal, where the challenges are quite daunting. This area is home to several tribal communities, including PVTGs, where socio-cultural taboos, economic constraints, and limited access to healthcare facilities work together to undermine awareness about adolescent health and hygiene (Chowdhury, 2021). Girls often face stigma around menstruation and other health issues, leading to absenteeism from school and reluctance to seek help. Moreover, infrastructural challenges, such as inadequate water and sanitation facilities, exacerbate the problem, hindering the adoption of healthy practices (Patra, 2020).

However, Non-Governmental Organizations (NGOs) play a pivotal role in addressing these critical gaps by implementing community-based health education programmes. Their grassroots approaches often include a deep focus on awareness campaigns, distribution of sanitary products, and training for local health workers. NGOs such as the CESR (Centre for Environmental and Socio-economic Regeneration) have been functioning to raise awareness, promote behavioural change, and engage stakeholders in tribal areas. By tailoring interventions to cultural contexts and involving community members, these organizations effectively bridge the gap left by conventional health education systems (Sinha & Das, 2022). Understanding and evaluating their efforts is crucial for scaling impactful strategies in similar underserved regions.

### *1.1 CESR NGO*

The Centre for Environmental and Socio-Economic Regeneration (CESR) is a non-governmental organization founded in 1993 in Kolkata. It focuses on environmental protection and the socio-economic development of tribal and economically marginalized communities. With expertise across agriculture, education, health, and women and child development, CESR's mission derives from the philosophy of promoting social justice, equity, and sustainable development.

CESR's initiatives span across diverse areas, with key programmes addressing critical needs; *please refer to Table 1*.

Through these impactful programmes, CESR continues to improve the lives of marginalized communities and foster inclusive development in rural India.

## 2 Rationale of the Study

Adolescence is a transformative period marked by rapid physical, psychological, and social changes, yet it remains one of the most neglected stages in health education, particularly in rural and tribal areas like Ayodhya Hill located in the faraway outskirts of Purulia town. With nearly 20.23% of Purulia's population being

**Table 1** Programmes or activities by CESR NGO

| Programme name | Objectives | Key activities | Impact/outreach |
|---|---|---|---|
| Supplementary Education Programme | Improve access to education for tribal children, reduce school dropouts | Learning centres, engaging and enjoyable teaching methods, targeting first-time learners | Improved education access for tribal children |
| Adolescent Intervention Programme | Reduce child marriage, adolescent pregnancies, and school dropouts | Health and rights awareness campaigns, community outreach, adolescent group formation | Reduced early marriage and adolescent pregnancies |
| Mobile Health Unit (MHU) | Provide essential medical services to remote communities | Diagnostics, treatment, preventive healthcare, mobile health unit visits | Improved health outcomes, better access to healthcare |
| Internet Sathi Project | Empower rural communities through digital literacy | Internet-enabled cycles, digital literacy training, community engagement | Digital literacy for over 800 villages |
| eVidyaloka Programme | Enhance education quality, support online learning | Live online classes, on-ground logistics, infrastructure maintenance, student engagement | Improved learning outcomes in 4 junior high schools |
| SABLA-Kanyashree Joint Convergence Programme | Empower adolescent girls, promote continued education, prevent early marriage | Adolescent girls' groups, skills training, self-esteem building, community meetings, Kanyashree and SABLA integration | Reached over 9000 girls, strengthened self-esteem and education |

*Source*: Compiled from CESR Official Website, https://cesrindia.org

adolescents, the lack of access to adequate health and hygiene education poses a significant challenge for their holistic development (Census, 2011). The situation gets exacerbated by socio-economic disadvantages, cultural taboos, and limited infrastructure, making it imperative to address this hiatus through innovative and community-driven approaches.

The Centre for Environmental and Socio-Economic Regeneration (CESR) has emerged as a critical player in bridging these gaps. Its Adolescent Intervention Programme in Baghmundi block focuses on preventing child marriage, promoting secondary education, and addressing health challenges like anaemia and malnutrition through awareness and capacity-building initiatives. These efforts align with global calls for action, as articulated by the World Health Organization, which emphasizes that "investing in adolescent health and well-being brings a triple dividend of benefits covering today, into adulthood, and for the next generation" (WHO, 2020).

This study was chosen to explore and analyse the effectiveness of CESR's initiatives in creating awareness and fostering behavioural changes among adolescents in the Ayodhya Hill region. By evaluating the CESR's strategies, including its collaboration with government schemes and grassroots engagement, this research aims to highlight the CESR's effective interventions and provide best practices for enhancing adolescent health education in similar contexts.

## 3 Research Objectives

I. To understand the CESR's strategies for promoting adolescent health and hygiene education among girls.
II. To identify challenges for implementing CESR's adolescent health and hygiene education initiatives among girls.

## 4 Research Questions

I. What are CESR's key programmes and strategies for adolescent health and hygiene education among girls?
II. What challenges does CESR face in implementing these initiatives?

## 5 Methodology

### *5.1 Research Design*

Here the researchers employed the exploratory research design.

### *5.2 Study Area*

Researchers selected the Baghmundi Block of Ayodhya Hill area, Purulia, West Bengal for this study.

### *5.3 Samples of the Study*

Here 20 adolescent girls, 20 community members, and 15 CESR program staff were selected as samples for this study.

### *5.4 Sampling Method*

The purposive sampling method was used for gathering the samples.

### 5.5 Data Collection Methods

I. Focus group discussions (FGDs) with community members.
II. Interviews with CESR coordinators and field workers and girls.
III. Observation of CESR's activities.

### 5.6 Data Analysis

Data were analysed through qualitative thematic analysis for interviews and FGDs.

## 6 Findings of the Study

### 6.1 Objective 1: To Understand the CESR's Strategies for Promoting Adolescent Health and Hygiene Education Among Girls

When the researchers interviewed the NGO's administrator, it became conspicuous that the Baghmundi block is experiencing limited access to healthcare facilities. Many adolescent girls face a harsh reality when it comes to menstrual health and hygiene. Without access to proper menstrual products, they are left with no choice but to use unsafe alternatives like cloth or even leaves. The situation worsens at school, where inadequate facilities make managing their periods difficult, causing them to miss classes regularly. This disrupts their education and denies them the chance to grow, learn, and realize their full potential, creating a cycle of inequality that deeply impacts their future. So, in these perspectives, the Centre for Environmental and Socio-Economic Regeneration has developed a series of innovative strategies aimed at promoting adolescent health and hygiene education among girls.

#### 6.1.1 Community-Based Awareness Programmes: A Platform for Change

The CESR's community-based awareness programmes play a pivotal role in addressing the stigma surrounding menstruation and promoting open conversations about adolescent health. These programmes focus on creating safe, inclusive spaces where girls and community members can discuss sensitive issues without fear of judgement. By collaborating with local leaders, grassroots organizations, and influencers, CESR facilitates collective responsibility for health education and challenges cultural misconceptions.

Through community engagement, CESR encourages the normalization of menstruation and the adoption of healthy hygiene practices. The use of storytelling and participatory methods fosters a supportive environment, where girls gain confidence and knowledge about menstrual hygiene. One participant shared her experience thus: "Before CESR came, we didn't know how to talk about periods. Now we can talk openly, and I feel more confident".

### 6.1.2 Affordable Access to Menstrual Hygiene Products: Bridging the Gap

To address the financial barriers that many families face in accessing menstrual products, CESR promotes affordable solutions by partnering with community groups and parents. The organization encourages local production and distribution networks for reusable cloth pads, menstrual cups, and biodegradable products. This approach not only ensures that girls have access to safe and cost-effective hygiene products but also alleviates the financial burden on families.

CESR's distribution of sanitary products and hygiene kits has proven to be a vital strategy in ensuring that tribal girls can manage their menstrual health effectively. This initiative is especially crucial in rural areas where sanitary products are often unavailable or unaffordable, allowing girls to continue their education and maintain their health.

### 6.1.3 Educational Workshops: Empowering Through Knowledge and Interactive Learning

The educational workshops of the CESR serve as a cornerstone of its health education initiatives. These workshops incorporate interactive and participatory techniques to engage adolescent girls in the learning process. Unlike traditional lecture-style education, CESR's workshops include role-playing, group discussions, and games that encourage active participation.

By creating a safe space for girls to discuss sensitive topics such as menstruation, sexual health, and mental well-being, CESR fosters an environment where girls feel comfortable asking questions and seeking guidance. As one participant noted, "I used to feel ashamed talking about my periods. But now, I feel confident asking about anything—like how to take care of myself better".

These workshops also cover a holistic range of topics, including nutrition, mental health, and life skills. Girls are educated and become sensitized about the importance of self-care, stress management, and emotional wellness, which are vital for overall health during adolescence. A participant shared, "We talk about how to stay calm when we feel stressed or sad. It's so helpful because school and life can sometimes be overwhelming".

### 6.1.4 Capacity Building for Project Staff and Community Facilitators: Ensuring Long-Term Sustainability

CESR's capacity-building initiatives aim to equip Project Staff and community facilitators with the knowledge, skills, and confidence necessary to teach adolescent health topics effectively. Many of them, especially in rural communities, have expressed discomfort in addressing topics like menstruation due to cultural taboos or lack of training. 7 days, CESR's training programmes provide them with the technical knowledge to address a wide range of adolescent health issues, ensuring that they can communicate these topics in an accurate and culturally sensitive manner.

By creating a safe and open environment for dialogue, CESR empowers teachers to become change agents within their communities. Teachers trained by CESR not only teach students but also act as mentors, supporting them through sensitive issues and providing the emotional support needed during adolescence. One teacher noted, "Before the training, I was uncomfortable talking about topics like menstruation. Now, I feel equipped to answer students' questions and provide the support they need".

### 6.1.5 Breaking the Silence and Dismantling Stigma: A Cultural Transformation

Historically, menstruation has been a subject of silence and shame in many conservative communities. CESR's initiatives work to dismantle this stigma through storytelling, puppet shows, folk songs, street dramas, peer discussions, and community engagement. The use of culturally relevant communication methods, such as storytelling by local women, helps normalize menstruation and builds solidarity among girls and community members.

By promoting open conversations and addressing the emotional and psychological aspects of menstrual health, CESR fosters a sense of community and support. The organization's peer network model allows girls to share experiences, ask questions, and learn from each other, reducing feelings of isolation. "We feel more comfortable talking about our periods now", shared one participant, highlighting the shift towards greater openness.

## 6.2 *Objective 2: To Identify Challenges for Implementing CESR's Adolescent Health and Hygiene Education Initiatives Among Girls*

Implementing the CESR's adolescent health and hygiene education initiatives among girls comes with several challenges that affect the programme's reach, effectiveness, and sustainability. These challenges can be categorized into social, cultural, economic, and logistical barriers. Below are the key challenges identified through research and feedback from participants:

### 6.2.1 Cultural and Social Stigma

#### 6.2.1.1 Menstrual Taboos and Gender Norms

One of the most significant challenges is the deep-rooted cultural stigma around menstruation and women's health in many communities. In this study, community members, especially elders and leaders, expressed discomfort with frankly discussing menstruation. A community leader shared that menstrual health is considered a "private matter" and should not be addressed publicly. This sentiment was echoed by several community members, who feared that discussing menstruation could lead to social unrest or challenge traditional norms. This makes it difficult to openly discuss and educate girls about menstrual health, as they may be discouraged from sharing their experiences.

#### 6.2.1.2 Gender Inequality

In some communities, gender norms dictate that girls should prioritize domestic chores over education, limiting their opportunities to engage in health education programmes. Another example of gender roles influencing participation in CESR's programmes comes from a conversation with a father in a rural community. A male parent shared, "Health education is good, but my daughter should be learning how to cook and clean. These are the skills she would need when she would get married. Health is secondary". This mindset, rooted in traditional gender expectations, prioritized domestic skills over personal health education, making it uphill for his daughter to attend the programme regularly. This belief reflects a broader cultural tendency to limit girls' opportunities to engage in education that goes beyond household responsibilities.

### 6.2.2 Lack of Awareness and Education

#### 6.2.2.1 Limited Knowledge of Health Issues

Many girls, particularly in rural and marginalized communities, lack basic knowledge about personal hygiene, menstruation, and reproductive health. Without prior understanding, girls might not recognize the importance of the information presented in CESR's programmes. Hence, the core challenge was the lack of basic knowledge about menstruation and personal hygiene. Here, the researchers find it opportune to share an incident during data collection, where a group of girls expressed confusion about menstrual cycles, having never been taught about it at home or school. Many girls struggled to understand the importance of menstrual hygiene, reducing their engagement in the educational sessions.

#### 6.2.2.2 Reluctance to Discuss Health Topics

Some girls may feel embarrassed or uncomfortable talking about their health, particularly reproductive and menstrual health. During interviews, it became evident that some girls were uncomfortable discussing health topics openly. This hesitation hindered their participation in the programmes. The researchers observed that girls would whisper to each other and avoid eye contact when asked about menstrual hygiene, indicating their discomfort with the topic. This reluctance can affect participation in programmes, making it difficult for CESR to effectively communicate the importance of health education.

### 6.2.3 Economic Barriers

#### 6.2.3.1 Inability to Afford Sanitary Products

Economic constraints are a major barrier to ensuring long-term participation in CESR's programmes. The researchers found how some families were unable to afford sanitary products, even though CESR provided hygiene kits during workshops. However, the kits were often seen as a temporary offering and girls shared that they had to use cloth or other alternatives due to the ongoing financial challenges.

### 6.2.4 Limited Access to Educational Resources

#### 6.2.4.1 Lack of Infrastructure and Facilities

In many rural areas, schools and communities may lack the infrastructure necessary to effectively support health education programmes. For example, there may not be clean water, sanitary facilities, or private spaces for girls to manage their menstrual health. Without these basic resources, it becomes more challenging to teach girls about proper hygiene practices.

#### 6.2.4.2 Inadequate Educational Materials

While CESR provides educational materials, some areas may suffer from a shortage of quality, age-appropriate resources that are easier for the girls to understand and relate to. In some instances, the materials provided may not be culturally relevant or available in the local language, limiting their impact.

### 6.2.5 Resistance from Community Leaders and Parents

#### 6.2.5.1 Lack of Support from Adults

In some cases, community leaders, parents, or caregivers may resist or be reluctant to embrace CESR's initiatives. This resistance can stem from cultural beliefs, lack of understanding about the importance of adolescent health education, or fear that discussing sensitive topics may disrupt traditional norms. This lack of support can hinder programme implementation and limit its reach.

#### 6.2.5.2 Parental Concerns

Some parents may fear that open discussions on topics like menstruation, sexuality, and emotional health could corrupt their children or encourage inappropriate behaviour. These fears can lead to reluctance to allow their daughters to participate in CESR's educational programmes, especially in areas where traditional views on sexuality and gender roles are prevalent.

### 6.2.6 Logistical Challenges

#### 6.2.6.1 Geographical Barriers

In rural and remote areas, geographical distance from CESR's centres or partner institutions can pose a significant challenge. Girls may find it difficult to travel long distances to attend workshops, and the lack of adequate transportation can create logistical obstacles.

#### 6.2.6.2 Scheduling Conflicts

Timing and availability of educational sessions can conflict with girls' other responsibilities, such as household chores, taking care of younger siblings, or attending school. This creates barriers to consistent participation in CESR's programmes, as girls may have competing priorities that prevent them from attending sessions regularly.

### 6.2.7 Sustainability and Long-Term Impact

#### 6.2.7.1 Dependence on External Funding

Many of CESR's initiatives depend on external funding and donations, which can limit the long-term sustainability of the programmes. Many NGO staff pointed out the financial limitations of the programmes, which impacted its sustainability. "Although we manage to distribute kits during workshops, the long-term availability of sanitary products is still a major concern. We cannot guarantee continuous supply", said one staff member. The reliance on external funding also posed a serious challenge to ensuring long-term programme viability and continuity.

#### 6.2.7.2 Programme Scalability

While CESR's initiatives have had a positive impact in the areas where they have been implemented, scaling the programme to reach more girls in different regions or communities requires additional resources, staff, and logistical coordination. This can be a significant challenge, particularly in areas where community resources and government support are limited.

### 6.2.8 Language and Communication Barriers

#### 6.2.8.1 Diverse Linguistic Landscape

In areas with linguistic diversity, language barriers can affect the effectiveness of CESR's health education programmes. Girls may speak different dialects or languages, making it difficult for teachers to communicate health information clearly and effectively. This can be particularly challenging in regions with multiple ethnic groups or when educational materials are not available in the local language.

### 6.2.9 Peer Pressure and Social Influences

#### 6.2.9.1 Influence of Peers and Friends

Adolescents are often heavily influenced by their peers, and in some cases, peer pressure can undermine the messages of health education programmes. During the data collection, one participant mentioned, “My friends told me it’s not okay to talk about menstrual health. They said it’s embarrassing”. This social pressure often interposes to create resistance among girls to fully engage with the programme, especially in settings where peers adhere to strict gender norms.

#### 6.2.9.2 Cultural Influence

Broader societal norms and pressures can also deter girls from embracing the health education provided by CESR. Girls expressed feeling embarrassed to talk about menstrual health, even in a group setting. One girl shared, “I felt shy at first, especially when we had to speak about it in front of others. It felt awkward like people would judge us”. This discomfort was particularly pronounced in communities where discussing menstruation was taboo. If their parents, community leaders, or peers do not value or support these programmes, it may be difficult for girls to feel motivated to learn and apply the knowledge they gain.

## 7 Discussion

CESR’s initiatives in Ayodhya Hill, Purulia, have demonstrated significant progress in addressing adolescent health and hygiene education gaps. Through a combination of community-based awareness programmes, educational workshops, peer education, and distribution of hygiene kits, CESR has contributed to improving knowledge and practices around menstrual hygiene, reproductive health, and emotional well-being. As Pandey et al. (2020) highlight, community-based interventions are pivotal in overcoming the silence surrounding menstruation, which is especially prevalent in rural areas. CESR’s strategy of engaging communities and fostering open discussions has proven effective in dismantling the stigma surrounding menstrual health. Educational workshops incorporating interactive methods like role-playing and group activities have been particularly impactful, as such methods are known to improve engagement and knowledge retention (Kumar & Singh, 2018). The peer education model, where older girls mentor younger ones, is another key strategy that has enhanced the programme’s reach, as it empowers both the teachers and the learners (Bhasin, 2019). Additionally, the distribution of hygiene kits addresses the financial barriers to menstrual products, a critical factor in keeping girls in school (WHO, 2021).

However, the study also reveals several significant challenges to the success of these initiatives. The cultural stigma around menstruation and reproductive health remains a major hurdle in rural areas, where such topics are often considered taboo, making open discussion difficult (Srivastava, 2021). Economic constraints further exacerbate the issue, as many families cannot afford sanitary products, limiting the sustainability of the programme (UNICEF, 2020). Logistical barriers, such as inadequate infrastructure and transportation, also hinder participation in rural communities (Goel & Desai, 2019). Finally, resistance from community leaders and parents rooted in traditional gender norms presents another challenge, slowing the acceptance of health education (Patel & Sharma, 2017). Overcoming these barriers will require continued community engagement and policy advocacy to ensure long-term success and sustainability.

## 8 Conclusion

Reflecting on CESR's efforts in Ayodhya Hill, Purulia, it is evident that the organization has made significant progress in addressing the gaps in adolescent health and hygiene education. The community-based awareness programmes, educational workshops, peer education, and distribution of hygiene kits have not only provided essential knowledge to girls but also empowered them to take charge of their health. The success of these initiatives lies in the ability to break down long-standing taboos around menstruation and reproductive health, creating a more open and supportive environment for adolescent girls. Through these programmes, CESR has fostered a sense of agency and confidence among the participants, who are now more equipped to manage their health with greater understanding and resources.

However, upon deeper reflection, it is clear that while CESR has made remarkable strides, the road ahead remains challenging. The persistent cultural stigma surrounding menstruation, economic constraints, and logistical barriers are formidable obstacles that need ongoing attention. Additionally, resistance from traditional structures, including parents and community leaders, presents a complex challenge in ensuring the sustainability of health education. These reflections point to the necessity of a holistic approach that goes beyond just providing knowledge—an approach that includes continued community engagement, policy advocacy, and capacity building. Only by addressing these deeper systemic challenges can CESR's initiatives have a lasting, transformative impact on adolescent health and hygiene education in the Ayodhya region.

## References

ASER Report. (2022). Annual status of education report. Retrieved from www.asercentre.org.

Bhasin, R. (2019). The impact of peer education on menstrual hygiene management: A rural perspective. *Journal of Adolescent Health Research, 14*(3), 56–62.

Centre for Environmental and Socio-Economic Regeneration (CESR). *Programmes and activities*. CESR Official Website. Retrieved from https://cesrindia.org/.

Chowdhury, R. (2021). Socio-cultural barriers to adolescent health in tribal communities of Purulia, West Bengal. *Indian Journal of Rural Health, 12*(4), 45–56.

Goel, R., & Desai, P. (2019). Challenges in delivering health education in rural India: a focus on infrastructure and access. *International Journal of Rural Development Studies, 11*(2), 89–104.

Kumar, A., & Singh, N. (2018). Innovative teaching methods in health education: Role-playing and group activities in improving adolescent knowledge. *Journal of Health Promotion, 6*(1), 23–29.

Pandey, M., Gupta, L., & Roy, S. (2020). Breaking the silence: Community-based approaches to menstrual health management in rural India. *Indian Journal of Community Health, 12*(4), 101–114.

Patel, D., & Sharma, R. (2017). The role of traditional gender norms in resisting health education in rural areas. *Journal of Gender Studies, 8*(3), 45–59.

Patra, S. (2020). Water, sanitation, and hygiene (WASH) challenges in rural Indian schools: A case study of West Bengal. *Journal of Public Health Research, 9*(2), 78–84.

Sinha, P., & Das, R. (2022). The role of NGOs in promoting health and hygiene in tribal areas: A case study of CESR in West Bengal. *Social Development Quarterly, 15*(1), 34–50.

Srivastava, A. (2021). Cultural taboos and menstrual health: A study of rural Indian communities. *Journal of Cultural Anthropology, 15*(2), 78–88.

UDISE Report. (2021). Unified district information system for education plus. Retrieved from www.udise.in.

UNICEF. (2019). State of the world's children report. Retrieved from www.unicef.org.

UNICEF. (2020). Menstrual health and hygiene management in India: Challenges and interventions. Retrieved from www.unicef.org/india.

WHO. (2020). Adolescent health and well-being: Global guidelines. World Health Organization. Retrieved from www.who.int.

WHO. (2021). Financial barriers in accessing menstrual products: A global perspective. World Health Organization. Retrieved from www.who.int.

# Empowering Women Through Workplace Wellness: A Bangladesh Perspective

**Fatema-Tuz-Zohora**

## 1 Introduction

Workplace wellness encompasses programs and policies aimed at enhancing the health, safety, and overall well-being of employees. Women's workplace wellness specifically addresses the distinct challenges that women encounter in their professional environments. It has become a critical component of organizational sustainability and employee productivity. In Bangladesh, women constitute a significant portion of the workforce across various sectors, making this issue particularly relevant.

The concept of workplace wellness is especially vital due to the unique challenges faced by women in work settings. These include health and safety risks, lack of supportive infrastructure, and instances of workplace discrimination. Establishing a secure and supportive work environment for women fosters equality, efficiency, and overall well-being. In countries like Bangladesh, where cultural and societal norms often shape workplace dynamics, implementing targeted strategies is essential to ensure that women feel safe, valued, and empowered in their roles.

Throughout history, both men and women have contributed significantly to human progress. The active participation of women in the workforce is a key indicator of a nation's development. In recent years, women's involvement in the workforce has increased substantially in Bangladesh, signifying positive societal and economic advancements.

Despite their critical contributions to major industries such as garment manufacturing, agriculture, and services, women often face challenges that undermine their physical, mental, and emotional well-being. These issues hinder not only their

Fatema-Tuz-Zohora (✉)
Department of Marketing, University of Barishal, Barishal, Bangladesh
e-mail: ftzohora@bu.ac.bd

 
S. Batra (ed.), *Socioeconomic Factors, Consumer Health, and Broader Well-Being*, Advances in Mental Health and Addiction, https://doi.org/10.1007/978-3-032-05634-4_2

personal and professional growth but also the broader economic and social progress of the country. Addressing these challenges by promoting a healthier workforce is essential for boosting productivity, empowering women, advancing gender equality, and driving national development.

### *1.1 Objective of the Study*

The study has the following objectives:

- To illustrate the current state of workplace wellness initiatives for women workers in Bangladesh.
- To identify the primary health, safety, and well-being challenges faced by women workers across various sectors in Bangladesh.
- To propose actionable strategies and policy recommendations for enhancing workplace wellness and empowering women in the workforce.

## 2 Literature Review

Workplace wellness programs have been widely recognized as crucial for improving employee productivity, reducing absenteeism, and fostering a supportive work environment. However, the specific challenges faced by women workers, particularly in developing countries like Bangladesh, have not been adequately addressed in many workplace wellness initiatives. This section reviews relevant literature on the topic to highlight existing knowledge, gaps, and the significance of empowering women through workplace wellness programs.

According to research, gender-sensitive workplace rules are essential for addressing the unique difficulties that women face in the workplace. According to the International Labor Organization (ILO), women frequently face systemic obstacles such as unequal pay, restricted opportunities for leadership positions, and insufficient safety precautions at work (ILO, 2020). Well-designed wellness initiatives that address the specific needs of women have demonstrated the ability to improve job satisfaction and support the success of organizations (Brown & Macdonald, 2019).

In Bangladesh, the ready-made garment (RMG) sector is a cornerstone of economic and social development, employing over 4 million workers, 60–80% of whom are women (BGMEA, 2022). Despite its significant contributions, the sector faces critical challenges, including poor health and safety conditions for female workers (Akhter et al., 2010). Research indicates that these challenges include inadequate wages, excessive working hours, lack of maternity benefits, and pervasive workplace harassment (Kibria, 2018).

Existing workplace wellness programs in Bangladesh are limited in scope and often fail to address gender-specific needs. For example, most garment factories lack proper sanitation facilities, mental health support, and childcare services, which disproportionately affect women managing professional and domestic responsibilities (Hossain et al., 2021). Unsafe working conditions, such as poor ventilation, chemical exposure, and non-ergonomic workspaces, further contribute to long-term health problems for women workers.

Gender-based discrimination and harassment remain widespread, with inadequate grievance mechanisms leaving women vulnerable to exploitation (Ferdous & Jahan, 2020). Although legal provisions for maternity leave exist, inconsistent enforcement and the absence of childcare facilities hinder women's workforce participation (Sarker et al., 2021). The dual burden of work and domestic responsibilities exacerbates stress, leading to mental health challenges such as anxiety and depression (Rahman et al., 2020).

Global research underscores the need for targeted empowerment initiatives. Studies reveal that empowerment-focused health promotion programs significantly improve women's resilience and well-being by addressing structural, individual, and community-level factors (Kar et al., 1999; MacDonnell et al., 2012). Family-centered education based on empowerment models has also demonstrated positive impacts on mental health, particularly for vulnerable groups such as older women (Someia et al., 2024). Incorporating inclusive infrastructure into workplace wellness programs can enhance gender equality by addressing physical and socio-economic needs. This approach not only facilitates education and economic opportunities but also creates safer environments that promote mental health and social inclusion (Alison, 2023).

Empowering women through workplace wellness aligns with global development objectives, including the United Nations Sustainable Development Goal 5 (Gender Equality). In Bangladesh, such programs can increase women's workforce participation, foster gender equity, and drive economic growth. Research shows that organizations investing in women-centric wellness initiatives benefit from higher employee retention, improved morale, and enhanced productivity (Khan & Akhter, 2022).

## 2.1 Gaps in Existing Literature

While there is considerable research on workplace wellness and women's empowerment, few studies integrate these topics specifically within the Bangladeshi context. Most existing literature focuses on either gender equality or occupational health but lacks a holistic approach that combines both elements. Additionally, there is limited empirical data on the long-term impact of workplace wellness programs on women workers in Bangladesh.

## 3 Methodology

This study employs a qualitative methodology, examining secondary data sourced from a variety of materials, including academic research, industry analyses, financial publications, magazines, newspapers, online platforms, and academic dissertations. Extensive reviews of records and documents maintained by both governmental and non-governmental entities, along with other reliable national and international sources, were conducted.

Additionally, the research integrates perspectives from case studies and interviews with key participants such as labor rights activists, human resources experts, and female workers in Bangladesh. A synthesis of both qualitative and quantitative data from corporate annual reports and other trustworthy sources was carried out for in-depth analysis.

The focus of the study is on sectors with a notable presence of women, specifically the ready-made garment (RMG) industry, agriculture, and the service sector. By connecting a variety of data and viewpoints, this research offers an extensive understanding of the obstacles and opportunities related to workplace wellness for women in Bangladesh.

## 4 Global Perspective on Women Workplace Wellness

The wellness of women in the workplace has emerged as an essential concern worldwide as organizations and governments strive to cultivate equitable, inclusive, and supportive settings. Focusing on women's wellness at work involves several aspects, such as physical health, mental wellness, gender equality, and career advancement. Although advancements have been made in many areas, obstacles remain, especially in developing countries where gender inequalities in employment are more evident.

As reported by the World Bank, approximately 50% of women worldwide are part of the labor force, compared to 80% of men. Women frequently encounter fewer formal employment opportunities and restricted opportunities for advancement in their careers or businesses. In addition, women generally receive lower wages than their male equivalents.

The significance of women's mental health in the workplace goes well beyond personal impact. It sends ripples through both the corporate sphere and society as a whole. When women are encouraged to take charge of their health and well-being, they can more effectively thrive in their professions, foster innovation, and play an active role in their communities. This creates a mutually beneficial scenario where employees, employers, and the nation collectively gain advantages.

According to research conducted from February 2023 to October 2024, Gallup found that 51% of working women in the USA reported experiencing considerable stress during a significant portion of the previous day (compared to 39% of men).

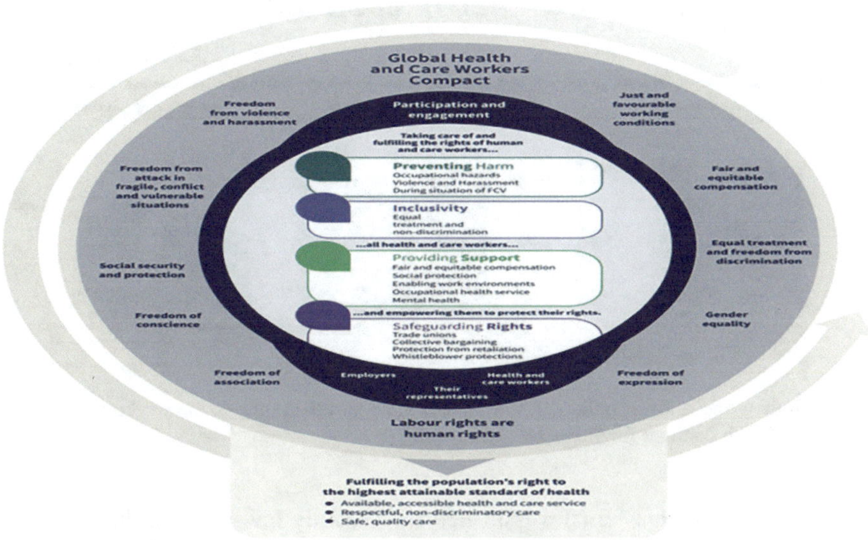


**Fig. 1** Global health and care worker compact. *Source*: World Health Organization (2023)

Additionally, 42% of working women indicated that their jobs have had either a somewhat or profoundly negative impact on their mental health over the past 6 months, in contrast to 37% of men. The resulting consequences of women's well-being have implications for organizations, as declines in well-being can lead to decreased engagement, increased burnout, and a rise in job-seeking behaviors.

Figure 1 shows that according to the World Health Organization (WHO), women make up nearly 70% of the worldwide health and care workforce, yet they occupy only 25% of leadership positions. This significant disparity in representation highlights persistent gender norms that minimize women's contributions and restrict their access to positions of power. At Women in Global Health, it is contended that leadership is essential for formulating policies that take into account the experiences of women workers. When women are not represented in leadership roles, decisions that impact their working conditions are made without their involvement, thereby reinforcing inequity.

A new report from the McKinsey Health Institute, which surveyed more than 30,000 workers in 30 different nations, found that women tend to feel more fatigued and suffer from poor mental and spiritual well-being compared to men, increasing their vulnerability to burnout. On a global scale, 42% of respondents indicated that they are experiencing symptoms of exhaustion. Nevertheless, women report exhaustion more frequently than men—46% compared to 38%, respectively. The largest disparities in exhaustion rates between genders were observed in France, India, Japan, the Netherlands, Nigeria, Saudi Arabia, and South Korea, where the difference exceeded 10%.

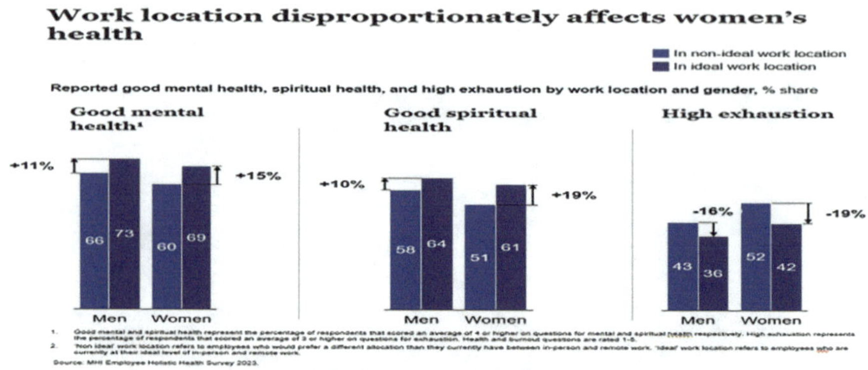


**Fig. 2** Women report lower holistic health across the board than men in the workplace. *Source*: McKinsey Health Institute Employment Survey (2023)

Figure 2 shows that females indicated significantly lower mental health levels than males, with 70% of men and 65% of women rating their mental health as good. Similarly, in terms of spiritual health, 61% of men and 56% of women indicated that they had good spiritual health. The connection between gender and mental health is extensively documented. On a global scale, women experience nearly double the lifetime prevalence of depression and most anxiety disorders in comparison with men.

The World Economic Forum's Healthy Workforces Initiative unites more than 50 prominent global organizations to emphasize the importance of mental health for employees in the workplace. Through cooperative efforts involving multiple stakeholders, the initiative highlights best practices, essential metrics, and the persuasive business rationale for companies to invest in comprehensive mental health programs and policies. This collaborative platform enables stakeholders to achieve meaningful advancements in enhancing the psychological well-being and safety of the current workforce on a large scale.

## 4.1 *Key Global Trends and Practices*

### 4.1.1 Gender Equality in Workplace

Promoting gender equality is essential for enhancing women's well-being in the workplace. The International Labor Organization (ILO) supports equal compensation, the elimination of harassment in the workplace, and the establishment of policies that encourage gender parity in leadership positions. Nations such as Iceland have taken the lead by requiring pay gap audits to tackle wage disparity.

### 4.1.2 Flexible Work Arrangements

Worldwide, flexible work policies have been put in place to assist women in managing their work and personal lives. In nations such as Sweden and the Netherlands, measures like parental leave, shorter working hours, and opportunities for remote work have greatly enhanced women's participation in the workforce and their general well-being.

### 4.1.3 Health and Safety Measures

In industrial sectors, especially within developing countries, female workers frequently face hazardous working conditions. Initiatives like Better Work, collaboration between the International Finance Corporation (IFC) and the International Labor Organization (ILO), have made substantial improvements to the working environments for women in garment factories in Vietnam and Cambodia. These initiatives have resulted in a decrease in workplace injuries and better access to healthcare services.

### 4.1.4 Mental Health and Stress Management

Tackling mental health challenges has emerged as a key focus in workplace wellness initiatives worldwide. For instance, in both the United States and Canada, companies have incorporated Employee Assistance Programs (EAPs) and included mental health counseling in their benefits offerings (WHO, 2022).

### 4.1.5 Workplace Harassment Policies

Global movements such as #MeToo have motivated organizations to adopt strict anti-harassment policies. Programs like the UN Women's Empowerment Principles offer guidelines for fostering a harassment-free workplace culture (UN Women, 2020).

### 4.1.6 Technology and Innovation

Digital platforms are transforming workplace wellness globally. For example, apps like SHE Health in India offer health consultations and wellness resources specifically designed for women, improving access to healthcare in remote areas.

### 4.1.7 Maternity and Childcare Support

Developed nations have implemented through maternity and childcare assistance programs, establishing worldwide standards for improving women's workplace health and participation in the workforce. Sweden and Norway, for instance, offer generous maternity leave and government-supported childcare services, allowing women to effectively manage both professional and family duties (OECD, 2021). In a similar vein, Japan provides subsidized childcare and extended maternity leave, enabling women to rejoin the workforce while fulfilling their family obligations.

Figure 3 illustrates which nations offer the most generous paid maternity leave benefits, measured by the number of weeks of full-rate compensation provided.

## *4.2 Regional Examples and Best Practices*

- **Europe:** Scandinavian countries are leading the way in implementing flexible work schedules and gender-neutral maternity leave laws. These initiatives have notably enhanced the participation of women in the workforce
- **Asia:** Nations such as Japan and South Korea are tackling conventional gender roles by fostering workplace diversity and enacting compulsory anti-discrimination legislation.
- **Africa:** In Kenya, programs such as the African Women in Agriculture Research and Development (AWARD) have concentrated on providing training and leadership development for female workers, thereby improving their well-being and advancing their career prospects (FAO, 2021).

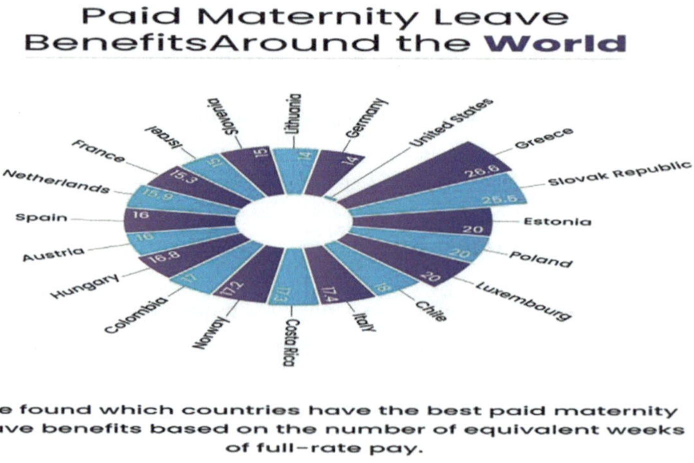


**Fig. 3** Paid maternity leave benefits around the world. *Source*: Cogent Info-tech (2023)

- **North America:** Organizations in the United States and Canada are implementing extensive wellness initiatives, which encompass mental health days, flexible work schedules, and childcare support, in order to retain female employees in the workforce.
- **UN Women's HeForShe Campaign:** A global initiative that encourages men and organizations to actively support gender equality.

## 5 Bangladesh Perspective on Women Workplace Wellness

Bangladesh now ranks 99th out of 146 economies in the World Economic Forum's (WEF) 2024 Global Gender Gap Index, dropping 40 points. For the 10th year in a row, it remains the leader in South Asia for gender equality despite the decline.

Figure 4 shows that as per the latest index Bangladesh has experienced the most significant drop from its earlier position of 59th in the global ranking. According to the research, this was mostly caused by the notable decline in the nation's economic gender parity over the previous 5 years. The gender disparity in the nation has now shrunk to 68.9%, down from 72.2% the year before. Despite the decline, Bangladesh has maintained its lead over other South Asian countries since surpassing Sri Lanka in 2014.

Figure 5 indicates that the WEF index evaluates the disparity between men and women in four key areas: political empowerment, health and survival, educational attainment, and economic participation and opportunity. These four areas are made up of 14 indicators. Nepal now ranks 117th globally, down from 116th the previous year, with the second-highest level of gender parity, with 66.4% of the gender gap

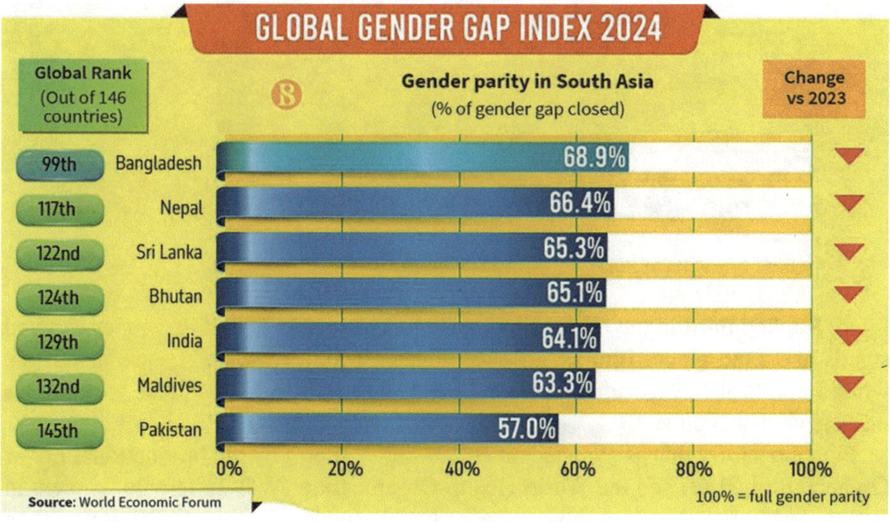


**Fig. 4** Global gender gap index. *Source*: World Economic Forum (2024)

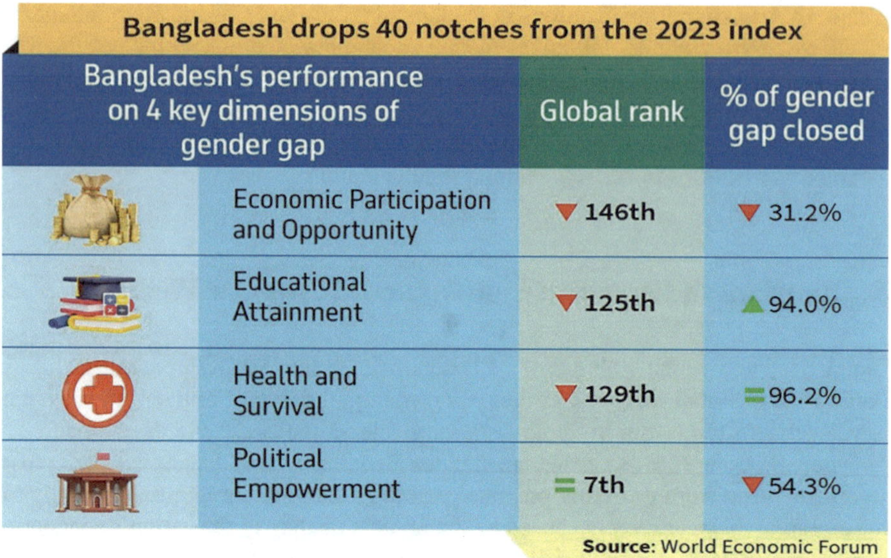

Bangladesh drops 40 notches from the 2023 index

| Bangladesh's performance on 4 key dimensions of gender gap | Global rank | % of gender gap closed |
|---|---|---|
| Economic Participation and Opportunity | ▼ 146th | ▼ 31.2% |
| Educational Attainment | ▼ 125th | ▲ 94.0% |
| Health and Survival | ▼ 129th | = 96.2% |
| Political Empowerment | = 7th | ▼ 54.3% |

**Source:** World Economic Forum

**Fig. 5** Bangladesh's performance on four key dimensions of gender gap. *Source*: World Economic Forum (2023)

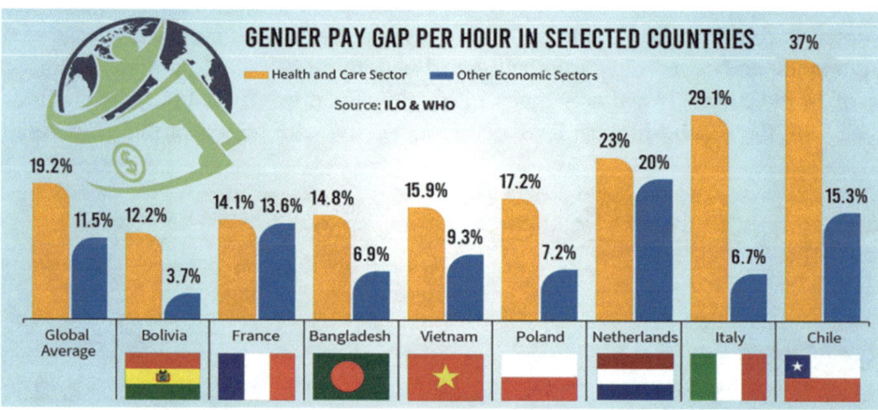


**Fig. 6** Gender pay gap per hour in selected countries. *Source*: info-graphic

filled. Ranked third in the region, Sri Lanka has closed 65.3% of its gender gap and stands at 122nd place. Bhutan follows closely at 124th with a closure of 65.1%, while India is at 129th with 64.1%, and the Maldives is in 132nd place with 63.3% of its gender gap closed.

Figure 6 shows that as per a recent collaborative report by the International Labor Organization (ILO) and the World Health Organization (WHO), female workers in Bangladesh's health and care sector earn hourly wages that are 14.8% lower than their male counterparts, while the wage gap in other sectors of the economy stands at 6.9%

Bangladesh is one of 18 nations where the average hourly gender disparity in the health and care sector is double that of other areas of the economy. The remaining countries include Brazil, Chile, Italy, Bolivia, Poland, and Vietnam.

## 5.1 *Initiatives and Progress*

### 5.1.1 Ready-Made Garment Sector Programs

The ready-made garment (RMG) industry stands as Bangladesh's foremost source of export revenue, with over 5000 garment factories in operation, providing jobs for more than four million individuals, of whom over 80% are women. The RMG sector is regarded as a cornerstone of the nation's economy, and one of its key strengths lies in its female workforce (Farhana et al., 2015).

According to Fig. 7, approximately 16,000 women are currently working as mid-level managers in Bangladesh's ready-made garment industry, which is the country's main sector for export earnings.

Programs such as Better Work Bangladesh, a collaborative effort by the ILO and IFC, have enhanced working conditions in the RMG industry, positively impacting thousands of female workers.

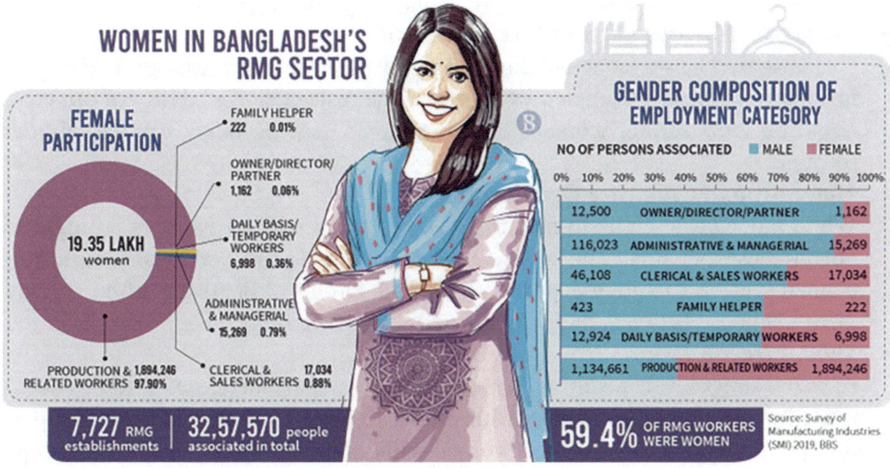


**Fig. 7** Women in Bangladesh RMG sector.

### 5.1.2 Government Policies

Labor laws mandate maternity leave and other gender-sensitive workplace measures, but enforcement continues to be a challenge.

### 5.1.3 NGO and Private Sector Efforts

NGOs such as BRAC and international organizations like CARE have launched programs to support women's health and well-being in workplaces. Some private companies are beginning to adopt gender-sensitive policies; however, these remain exceptions rather than the norm.

### 5.1.4 Awareness Campaigns

Public awareness campaigns focusing on workplace harassment, gender equality, and mental health are gaining traction in urban areas.

## 6 Findings

The report highlights several key findings:

- ***Health and Safety Concerns:***
  Female workers in Bangladesh frequently encounter substandard working conditions, which include inadequate sanitation, exposure to harmful substances, workplace toxins, and ergonomic issues. There is also a high prevalence of repetitive strain injuries due to physically demanding roles and unsafe environments.
- ***Workplace Harassment and Discrimination:***
  Gender-based harassment and discriminatory practices are prevalent, posing significant obstacles to women's well-being. The restricted availability of effective reporting tools further worsens these problems, leaving many women without recourse.
- ***Maternity and Childcare Deficiencies:***
  While labor laws stipulate maternity leave, many women workers struggle to obtain these benefits. The absence of on-site childcare services complicates women's efforts to juggle professional and family obligations, often forcing them to choose between their careers and caregiving roles.
- ***Mental Health Issues:***
  Elevated stress levels resulting from both professional and domestic duties negatively impact women's mental health. However, workplace mental health support programs are quite rare, leaving women without the necessary resources to cope with stress and emotional difficulties

- ***Limited Access to Wellness Programs:***
  In Bangladesh, there are few workplaces that have established comprehensive wellness programs specifically designed for the needs of women workers. There is a notable deficiency in gender-sensitive initiatives that cater to both physical and mental health needs, which hinders women's overall health and productivity.

### *6.1 Originality/Value*

This report contributes to the understanding of workplace well-being by focusing specifically on working women in Bangladesh, an area that is often overlooked. It highlights the particular challenges they face and underline the importance of implementing targeted well-being programs. The findings and recommendations are valuable for policymakers, employers, and advocacy groups aiming to create equitable workplaces that empower women.

### *6.2 Research Limitations/Implications*

The findings of the report mainly rely on secondary data and qualitative insights, which may limit the scope and generalizability of the findings.

- Quantitative research or surveys might offer more profound understanding of the occurrence and effect of workplace wellness initiatives on women workers.
- Future studies might investigate the long-term impact of implemented wellness strategies across various sectors in Bangladesh.

## 7 Implications

### *7.1 Practical Implications*

#### 7.1.1 Policy Recommendations

- Enhance and enforce labor laws regarding workplace health, safety, and maternity support.
- Implement and enforce measures to prevent and address workplace harassment while promoting gender equality.

### 7.1.2 Infrastructure Development

- Ensure the availability of secure and private sanitation facilities designed for women's requirements.
- Create on-site childcare centers and breastfeeding-friendly areas to assist working mothers.
- Upgrade workstations by investing in ergonomic designs and safety gear.

### 7.1.3 Wellness Programs

- Introduce regular health check-ups, mental health assistance programs, and nutrition awareness initiatives.
- Provide gender-sensitivity training for both staff and management to cultivate a respectful and inclusive workplace environment.

### 7.1.4 Technology Integration

- Develop and implement mobile platforms that allow women workers to report harassment confidentially and access wellness resources conveniently.

### 7.1.5 Collaborative Efforts

- Foster partnerships between government, private sector, and NGOs to design and implement gender-sensitive workplace wellness initiatives

## *7.2 Social Implications*

Focusing on the well-being of women in the workplace provides considerable social benefits. It promotes gender equality by tackling systemic obstacles that restrict women's involvement in the labor market. Improved wellness initiatives can economically empower women, decrease poverty rates, and enhance the overall health of families and communities. Additionally, promoting a healthier workforce aids in national economic growth and reinforces social unity.

## 8 Conclusion

Empowering women through workplace wellness is a moral imperative and a strategic necessity for fostering economic growth, gender equality, and sustainable development in Bangladesh. A significant part of the workforce consists of women across various sectors, yet they still encounter obstacles that hinder their physical, mental, and emotional well-being. It is vital to address concerns such as unsafe working conditions, workplace harassment, insufficient maternity leave and childcare assistance, and restricted access to wellness initiatives in order to establish an inclusive and fair work environment.

Global best practices, exemplified by Scandinavian nations and initiatives like Better Work, illustrate that well-directed policies, robust infrastructure, and awareness initiatives can greatly improve women's well-being in the workplace. In Bangladesh, the implementation of labor regulations, investment in infrastructure, and the promotion of partnerships among the government, private sector, and nongovernmental organizations can lead to significant transformative progress.

By emphasizing the importance of women's wellness in the workplace Bangladesh can improve workforce productivity and empower women to achieve their full potential, thereby contributing to national progress and aligning with global sustainability goals. Addressing the challenges faced by women workers requires a multifaceted approach that incorporates health and safety measures, mental health support, maternity benefits, and anti-discrimination policies. Future research should aim to bridge the identified gaps by exploring the effectiveness of such initiatives across different sectors in Bangladesh. The insights and suggestions of this report serve as a roadmap for policymakers, employers, and advocacy groups to create a healthier, safer, and more inclusive future for women workers in the country.

## References

Akhter, S., Salahuddin, A. F. M., Iqbal, M., Malek, A. B. M. A., & Jahan, N. (2010). Health and occupational safety for female workforce of garment industries in Bangladesh. *Journal of Mechanical Engineering, 41*(1), 65–70.

Alison, R. (2023). Empowering women through inclusive infrastructure: Implications for wellbeing. *Journal of International Social Research, 16*(102).

Avais, M. A., Wassan, A., & Shah, S. (2014). A case study on problems of working women in city Sukkur. *Academic Research International, 5*(2).

Bakari, R. (2022). Meeting the need of help-seekers with an empowerment model: A shift in emotional wellness. *Horizon Journal of Humanities & Social Sciences Research, 4*(1), 25–36.

BGMEA. (2022). Women in the RMG sector: Contributions and challenges.

Brown, A., & Macdonald, T. (2019). The impact of wellness programs on job satisfaction and organizational success. Retrieved December 25, 2024, from https://www.cogentinfo.com/resources/wellness-at-work-how-employers-in-the-us-can-champion-womens-health.

Cogent Infotech. (2023). Wellness at work: How employers in the US can champion women's health. Retrieved December 24, 2024, from https://www.cogentinfo.com/resources/wellness-at-work-how-employers-in-the-us-can-champion-womens-health.

Correll, S. J., & Benard, S. (2006). Biased estimators? Comparing status and statistical theories of gender discrimination. In *Advances in group processes* (pp. 89–116). Emerald.

D'Souza, M. S., Karkada, S. N., Somayaji, G., & Venkatesaperumal, R. (2013). Women's well-being and reproductive health in Indian mining communities: Need for empowerment. *Reproductive Health, 10*, 1–12.

Farhana, K., Syduzzaman, M., & Munir, M. S. (2015). Present status of workers in ready-made garments industries in Bangladesh. *European Scientific Journal, 11*(7).

Ferdous, R., & Jahan, S. (2020). Gender-based discrimination in Bangladeshi workplaces.

Food and Agriculture Organization (FAO). (2021). Empowering women in agriculture. Retrieved from www.fao.org

Green, J., & Hand, J. R. (2024). McKinsey's diversity matters/delivers/wins results revisited. *Econ Journal Watch, 21*(1).

Hossain, A., et al. (2021). Gender-specific challenges in workplace wellness programs in Bangladesh.

Hossain, R. (2022). Story of country's first female manager in RMG. Retrieved December 25, 2024, from https://www.tbsnews.net/women-empowerment/story-countrys-first-female-manager-rmg-381481.

https://www.gallup.com/workplace/653843/program-culture-women-wellbeing-work.aspx

International Labour Organization (ILO). (2020). Gender equality at the heart of decent work. Retrieved from www.ilo.org.

Kar, S. B., Pascual, C. A., & Chickering, K. L. (1999). Empowerment of women for health promotion: A meta-analysis. *Social Science & Medicine, 49*(11), 1431–1460.

Khan, M., & Akhter, S. (2022). The economic impact of women-centric wellness initiatives.

Kibria, S. (2018). Challenges facing women workers in Bangladesh.

MacDonnell, J. A., Dastjerdi, M., Bokore, N., & Khanlou, N. (2012). Becoming resilient: Promoting the mental health and well-being of immigrant women in a Canadian context. *Nursing Research and Practice, 2012*(1), 576586.

McKinsey Health Institute Employment Survey. (2023). Women report lower holistic health across the board than men in the workplace. Retrieved December 27, 2024, from https://www.mckinsey.com/mhi/our-insights/reframing-employee-health-moving-beyond-burnout-to-holistic-health.

Nahr, M. S. S. (2024). Bangladesh slips 40 notches in global gender equality ranking. Retrieved December 25, 2024, from https://www.tbsnews.net/bangladesh/bangladesh-slips-40-notches-global-gender-equality-ranking-875646.

OECD. (2021). Parental leave systems across OECD countries. Retrieved from www.oecd.org.

Rahman, T., et al. (2020). The dual burden of professional and domestic responsibilities in Bangladesh.

Sarker, R., et al. (2021). Maternity leave policies and childcare support in Bangladesh.

Someia, N. M., Atri, S. B., Areshtanab, H. N., Farshbaf-Khalili, A., & Babaie, S. (2024). The efficacy of training based on the family-centered empowerment model on the mental health of aged women: A stratified randomized controlled trial. *BMC Women's Health, 24*(1), 599.

UN Women. (2020). Women's empowerment principles. Retrieved from www.unwomen.org.

Vidmar, R. J. (1992). On the use of atmospheric plasmas as electromagnetic reflectors. *IEEE Transactions on Plasma Science, 21*(3), 876–880. http://www.halcyon.com/pub/journals/21ps03-vidmar

Womeningh. (2024). Feminist insights on the global health workers compact: Women in global health's perspective. Retrieved December 22, 2024, from https://womeningh.org/feminist-insights-on-the-global-health-workers-compact-women-in-global-healths-perspective/.

World Economic Forum. (2024). Prioritizing the health of female employees is a strategic imperative. Here are 4 ways to do it. Retrieved December 26, 2024, from https://www.weforum.org/stories/2024/03/womens-mental-health-is-a-strategic-imperative-heres-how-employers-can-bolster-it-today/.

World Health Organization (WHO). (2022). Mental health in the workplace. Retrieved December 28, 2024, from https://www.who.int/publications/i/item/9789240053052.

World Health Organization (WHO). (2023). Global health and care worker compact. Retrieved December 29, 2024, from https://cdn.who.int/media/docs/default-source/health-workforce/global-health-care-worker-compact.pdf?sfvrsn=5547f5c7_3&download=true.

Zaman. (2022). Bangladeshi women in health and care paid much less than in other sectors. Retrieved December 28, 2024, from https://www.tbsnews.net/bangladesh/health/more-women-work-health-and-care-earn-24-less-men-un-458342.

# Relationship Between Socio-Economic Determinants and Mental Health of Urban Population: A Gender-Based Analysis

**Kamalika Dasgupta, Sanchita De, Lalima Mukherjee, and Soumi Datta**

## 1 Introduction

As per the predictions of the United Nations Population Division, by 2030, the developing world will have more people living in urban areas than in rural areas and by 2050, two-thirds of all developing countries' total population will probably be urban. India will not be an exception to this trend. In India approximately 28% of the population lives in cities, which has increased to 41% by the year 2020. Urbanization has its own advantages and disadvantages. Although it has social disparities and insecurities, insufficient association with nature and exposure to pollution of different kinds are some of the significant factors affecting the health of urban population in totality and mental health to be specific. There is countless evidence about the correlation between urbanization and deteriorating mental health. Rapid urbanization is resulting in speedy increase in the urban population as a fraction of total population of the world. By the end of 2030, it is believed that the majority of the global population will live in cities. This is a huge paradigm shift in the human population dynamics and it has been drawing the attention of most of the world's nations' economies. It has become a grave concern as the influence of urbanization on mental health is undeniable.

K. Dasgupta (✉)
Institute of Engineering & Management, University of Engineering and Management, Department of BBA, Kolkata, India

S. De · S. Datta
Institute of Engineering & Management, University of Engineering and Management, Department of Basic Science and Humanities, Kolkata, India

L. Mukherjee
Amity University, Amity Institute of Liberal Arts, Mumbai, India

 
S. Batra (ed.), *Socioeconomic Factors, Consumer Health, and Broader Well-Being*, Advances in Mental Health and Addiction, https://doi.org/10.1007/978-3-032-05634-4_3

Thus, the role of the urban setting in determining the health of the population requires attention to different characteristics of the urban surroundings that influence the mental health of the population. When the gender aspect is considered in the framework of socio-economic determinants of mental health, it generally refers to women's position in society and the widening gender gap in health outcomes, access to health services, access to educational and economic activities, etc.

The effect of urbanization is seen in women taking on non-conventional roles which were traditionally outside their sphere, along with traditional womanly roles. Thus, various studies indicate that as a result of urbanization women are much more aware of their potentials and are coming out of the household for jobs, for small business, to be financially independent. They are constantly in a position to prove their worth in a society shaped by patriarchy and at the same time performing the duties of being a wife, a mother, running the family, caring for the sick relatives and working outside. As a cherry on the cake, these multiple roles are often coupled with domestic violence, sexual abuse as well as financial exploitation. These factors create a feeling of inadequacy and helplessness among urban women.

Keeping in mind the association between rapid urbanization and the increasing risks of mental health issues, it becomes vital to investigate deeply into the consequences of such challenges. The social and personal factors reveal the beliefs, characteristics, and thought processes that empower or limit women in making decisions related to their own health. There are many social determinants that prevent women from participating in healthy behaviors. Personal causes such as concerns about privacy and time are some of them.

As a result, we can infer that urban settings, as compared to rural living, are associated with a greater risk of serious mental disorders among women more than men, which is vital to address because the world is getting urbanized faster than ever before. Urban environments and their landscapes, designs, and features impact mental health and well-being severely.

## 2 Survey of Literature

R.N. Bhardwaj (2019) assesses a few socio-economic determinants which potentially contribute to the existence of the issue related to mental health disorders in OECD countries. The approach that has been used on cross-sectional data is the Partial Least Square Approach. This paper focuses on the different structural determinants, for example, youth poverty, uncertainty in employment generation, inefficiencies in healthcare services, wealth inequality, and poverty. It also attempts to establish a connection between mental illness and use of different addictive substances, with a focus on youth population. The result emphasizes on the significance of addressing the social inequalities and promoting population-based preventive interventions, mainly during the critical life stages like the early childhood stages to reduce this issue regarding mental health disease mainly among the children, adolescents, young adults.

Sinha et al. (2023) in their paper have focused on different mental health issues like depression, anxiety, and stress among the women living in urban slum areas of Jaipur. The paper also seeks to find the determinants impacting them in this regard. In this paper, DASS-21 (Depression Anxiety Stress Scale) tool and other statistical methods were used and it was found that anxiety is the most common symptom (38.22%) compared to other symptoms like depression (18.61%) and stress (9.11%), particularly among women who were widowed or separated due to various social issues. The research finds a positive correlation between higher DASS scores and a few possible determinants such as inadequate sleep, pain, and lack of physical activity. The paper focuses on the importance of this issue to get addressed from the very beginning through better healthcare services in those areas.

Kirkbride et al. (2024) emphasize how an unfavorable social condition can intensify the helplessness to poor mental health throughout the life of the people who are exposed to such vulnerable situations. This paper seeks to present a roadmap for recognizing different social factors that can lead to mental health issues. Supportive evidence indicates that determinants are linked to the mental health outcomes. The paper also offers recommendations for improving the mental health conditions of the said population with the help of a preventive framework and reducing inequalities.

Maestre-Miquel et al. (2021) assessed the role of differences in gender in initiating mental health-related issues, depression, stress, anxiety, etc. through data analysis from 2017 survey. The paper found that there is always a high probability that women suffer more from mental health related issues as compared to men. Age, marital status, health conditions, etc. are considered to be the determinants which can cause such issues.

Arvind et al. (2019) focused on assessing the frequency, patterns, and the treatment gaps of mental disorders through a survey. It was found that women are more vulnerable than others in this regard. This emphasizes the importance of strengthening the mental health-related services so that the problem can be mitigated.

Shidhaye and Patel (2010) examined the interrelation among different socio-economic factors, gender, and health-related factors with Common Mental Disorders (CMDs) among married women living in rural areas of India. It was found that women are experiencing CMDs. There are few risk factors that can lead to severe mental health issues among women, including low levels of education, severe poverty, violence by intimate partner, dissatisfaction related to dowry, and excessive alcohol use.

Assari (2017) seeks to find the interaction among gender, race, and socio-economic status that affects MDE among American adults. Through data analysis, the paper finds an association between race and income with the presence of gender influencing the significance of income in this matter. It has been found that mental health outcomes may vary across different social communities.

Villatoro et al. (2017) focused on the intersection among race, ethnicity, socio-economic status, and gender regarding their influence on the importance of mental health care in the USA among adults. The paper found that the minorities (both racial and ethnic) use such mental health services less frequently, as they are often unaware of their importance. Therefore, the paper demonstrates how different types of social identities can affect people's perspective about mental health.

Albizu-Garcia et al. (2001) examined the issue of gender differences in case of mental health-related service usage. The paper used Andersen's Socio Behavioral Model and, after conducting the data analysis, found that both male and female used theses services at same rates, and gender does not play a significant role to affect the service usage while accounting for other factors as well. Surprisingly, while the poor mental health of men got reported, they sought care as well. The authors emphasized the importance of considering gender-specific factors when developing equitable good access to mental health services for deprived communities.

## 3 Objective of the Study

The objective of this research is to study the impact of different socio-economic determinants on the mental health of urban population, with special focus on gender roles. It aims to capture how various economic variables such as income, education, job status, and housing conditions, affect mental well-being, particularly for women, who frequently face challenges such as discrimination and limited opportunities. The existing literature on socio-economic determinants influencing mental well-being of urban population, particularly with additional importance on gender roles, discloses an interaction between different economic factors and distinctive challenges faced by women. Interestingly, the income disparities disproportionately affect women, creating significant obstacles to their mental well-being, generating symptoms like stress, anxiety, and depression. In spite of remarkable progress in education among urban communities, the gender pay gap still persists, restricting the financial independence and equal access to mental health resources for women, thereby increasing the mental health challenges. Additionally, improvements in women's educational attainment create extra liabilities for them. Employed women get engaged in unpaid domestic labor service along with their formal employment. This dual burden reduces their leisure time and self-care opportunities, contributing to prolonged stress, anxiety, and depression. Women often get employment in high-risk sector offering limited security and benefits which may further leave them vulnerable to workplace discrimination and harassment. All these bad experiences adversely affect their mental well-being, compounding the challenges posed by gendered expectations. Housing conditions also play a crucial role in determining mental health, particularly for women. People belonging to lower socio-economic strata generally lead an unstable and unsafe life. Moreover, women facing domestic violence may also suffer from long-term mental health consequences. The lack of safe housing options also increases their stress levels and feelings of isolation. The traditional gender role commands that women usually give priority to the well-being of their family members, sacrificing their own needs and mental health, which can disseminate cycles of anxiety and depression. Addressing these issues requires comprehensive policy measures which promote equal pay-scale, heighten equal access to socio-economic opportunities, support balanced work–life dynamic, ensure safe housing, and ultimately guarantee mental well-being to all individuals, regardless of gender. This study aims to address this issue of gender bias to foster an environment conducive to mental well-being for all. Finally, this analysis highlights the significance of a gender-sensitive approach in mental health research. Furthermore, this paper also seeks to explore differences in mental health outcomes across diverse urban communities and provide some policy suggestions to enhance mental health equity among all.

### *3.1 Research Questions*

(a) How do socio-economic determinants such as income, education, employment, and housing affect mental well-being among urban populations, particularly across gender lines?
(b) What is the correlation between low socio-economic status and the occurrence of mental health issues in urban communities which results in gender inequality?

## 4 Data and Methodology

Primary data were obtained from a diverse socio-economic background (income, nature of employment, etc.) of the urban population in the city of Kolkata to avoid the possibility of bias. A convenience sampling method has been employed for this purpose. At the outset of this section, we will highlight some key features of the data before framing our hypotheses and decide upon the methodology. The pilot study comprises 77 responses, of which 65% (approximately 51 respondents) are female. The data captures different socio-economic background of the respondents and the parameters of their mental health. Majority of the respondents are under 30 years of age and have a post-graduate degree. But interestingly almost half of the respondents (49.5%) are unemployed. This indicates one of the most important problems of any developing nation—educated unemployment, especially among urban women, which is an important economic source of mental ill-health as per the existing literature. Majority of our female respondents have higher educational qualification as compared to their male counterparts and most of them are working professionals as well (either in public or private enterprises). The average time to travel to the workplace is also higher for females than for male respondents. Most of the respondents have number of heads within four in their families, irrespective of gender. Another interesting aspect of the data shows that 18 out of 77 people have considered the option of therapy or counselling to improve their mental health, of which 72% are women. Also, 66 out of 77 respondents have reported that they suffer from anxiety quite often and 71% of them are women. This clearly indicates that urban women are the worst sufferers of mental ill-health and this outcome is also perfectly consistent with available literature.

**Table 1** Socio-economic parameters

| Parameters | Description |
|---|---|
| Gender | Male, Female, prefer not to say |
| Age | In years |
| Educational Qualification | High School, Graduate, Post Graduate, Doctorate, and others |
| Employment Status | Whether employed full time, part time, or unemployed |
| Population Density | Whether the population density of the residing area is low, moderate, or high |
| Avg. Monthly Household Income | In INR |
| Sector of Employment | Public, Private, Entrepreneur, etc. |
| Travel Time | Time required to travel to workplace |
| Earning Member | Whether they are the only earning member in the family |
| No. of heads | How many people are there in the family |
| Community/Organization | Whether engaged with any community or organization for socialization |
| Savings/Investment | Whether enough savings or investments are made |

*Source*: Authors' questionnaire

**Table 2** Mental health parameters

| Parameters | Description |
|---|---|
| Happiness | On a scale of 1–5 how satisfied you are at present? |
| Anxiety | How often do you feel anxious or depressed? |
| Therapy/Counselling | Have you ever considered taking therapy? Yes/No |
| Sleeping Behavior | How often do you find it hard to fall asleep? |
| Indecisiveness | How often do you struggle to focus and take decisions? |
| Self-Care | Have you ever considered any self-care (such as yoga, exercise, etc.) to improve your mental health condition? |

*Source*: Authors' questionnaire

Tables 1 and 2, respectively, depict the descriptions of socio-economic and mental health parameters considered for our study.

In the next step we create a composite mental health index to ease our analysis. The score of the index reflects the mental health status of the respondents. Higher index scores indicate better mental health status. A principal component analysis (PCA) was carried out to construct the index. Table 3 depicts the PCA results. Eigenvalues of each of the parameters were considered as weights during composition of the index.

From Table 3, it is clear that out of the six components of mental health considered, the feeling of happiness or satisfaction with current life has the highest importance, and efforts to improve mental health have the least importance in constructing of the index. After careful examination of the data gathered and a thorough survey of relevant literature available, we construct the following two hypotheses:

**Table 3** PCA results

| Parameters | Eigen values |
|---|---|
| Happiness | 1.97 |
| Anxiety | 1.27 |
| Therapy/Counselling | 0.98 |
| Sleeping Behavior | 0.73 |
| Indecisiveness | 0.56 |
| Self-Care | 0.46 |

*Source*: Authors' calculation

- ***Hypothesis 1*:** Female urban population suffers more from mental ill-health compared to the male urban population
- ***Hypothesis 2*:** The impact of socio-economic factors on mental ill-health differs for urban male and female population

In order to test the hypotheses we employ two non-parametric tests. The Wilcoxon rank-sum test is employed when we want to compare two related samples of unequal sizes to find out whether their population mean ranks are different from each other. It's particularly useful for testing Hypothesis 1. On the other hand, the MANOVA (Multivariate Analysis of Variance) is employed to analyze multiple dependent variables simultaneously to see if there are differences among groups based on one or more independent variables. Hence these techniques are particularly useful for testing Hypothesis 2.

## 5 Findings

For the first hypothesis, we want to check whether the male and the female urban population have the same average mental health index score or if it differs. If it differs, then we can certainly say that female population suffers more from mental ill-health compared to their male counter parts. The null hypothesis for the test would be as follows:

$$H_0 : avg\_mental\_health\_score\_men = avg\_mental\_health\_score\_women$$

In the test (the result of which is displayed in Table 4) gender is considered as the categorical variable. The male gender (smaller sample) is coded with 0 and the female gender (larger sample) is coded with 1. The *p*-value of the test statistic is 0.017, i.e. less than 0.05 and 0.10. This indicates that we reject $H_0$ and conclude that there is significant difference between the mental health of male and female urban population.

For the second hypothesis, we want to check whether all the socio-economic factors have an equal impact on male and female mental health. This is a justified proposition given the available literature. For example, time to travel from home to workplace might not affect men and women the same way. Greater travel times are

**Table 4** Wilcoxon rank-sum test results

| Gender | Observations | Rank sum | Expected |
|---|---|---|---|
| 0 | 27 | 1173 | 1053 |
| 1 | 50 | 1830 | 1950 |
| Combined | 77 | 3003 | 3003 |
| $Z = 1.350$, Prob > $\|Z\| = 0.017$ | | | |

*Source*: Authors' calculation

**Table 5** MANOVA results

| Source | Statistic | Value | $F$ | Prob > $F$ |
|---|---|---|---|---|
| Gender | Wilks' Lambda | 0.5958 | 4.01 | 0.000 |
| | Pillai's trace | 0.4042 | 4.23 | 0.045 |
| | Lawley-Hotelling Trace | 0.6785 | 5.09 | 0.023 |
| | Roy's Largest Root | 0.6785 | 4.01 | 0.019 |
| Residual | | 75 | | |

*Source*: Authors' calculation

likely to impact women more than men in a typical societal setup (ruling out all the exceptions) as women are expected to do all the household chores after returning from work. This might be a cause for stress and depression. Another instance can be the number of heads in the family. It can also affect women more than it does men. More family members or a larger family indicates higher dependency, greater time allotted to caregiving (as per our typical societal structure where women of the house are seen as caregivers too), which can lead to anxious behavior, sleep disorders, and even inability to take decisions. These are just two basic instances among many. Thus, we will perform MANOVA (Multivariate Analysis of Variance) for the socio-economic indicators to determine if their effects differ across genders. Table 5 exhibits the MANOVA results.

From the MANOVA results displayed above it is clear that all the four test statistics' *p*-values are significant. Wilks' Lambda is significant at 5, 1, and 10% level of significance. And the remaining three test statistics are significant at 5 and 10% level of significance. This indicates that there are significant differences in the dependent variables combined across groups. Thus clearly all the socio-economic indicators of our study have different impacts on the mental health across genders. The same indicator has very different (sometimes even opposite) impacts on the mental health of women and men.

## 6 Conclusion

From the above study, it is clear that happiness is the most important element for any human being. The point to be understood is that as per the above analysis, women face more anxiety due to their over-engagement with all kinds of work in the workplace as well as at home. The most alarming point is that women are probably the ones who don't have time to think about themselves, and since the advent of urbanization has not changed society's perception of women in terms of their work role, self-care is almost absent. Thus, the focus should be on the impact of mental health on women due to the changing social and occupational structure. A clear division of gender roles between men and women is essential in order to arrest the continuous increase in mental health problems among women. Actually, women are the worst victims of rapid urbanization as it has increased their responsibility without taking care of the dual role they are forced to play since they become adults. Policy makers need to delve deep into this matter and come out with proper formulated roles to protect future generations of women from increasing mental health problems.

## References

Albizu-Garcia, C. E., Alegría, M., Freeman, D., & Vera, M. (2001). Gender and health services use for a mental health problem. *Social Science & Medicine, 53*(7), 865–878. https://doi.org/10.1016/s0277-9536(00)00380-4

Arvind, B. A., Gururaj, G., Loganathan, S., Amudhan, S., Varghese, M., Benega, V., Rao, G. N., Kokane, A. M., Chavan, B. S., Dalal, P. K., Ram, D., Pathak, K., Lenin Singh, R. K., Singh, L. K., Sharma, P., Saha, P. K., Ramasubramanian, C., Mehta, R. Y., & Shibukumar, T. M. (2019). Prevalence and socioeconomic impact of depressive disorders in India: Multisite population-based cross-sectional study. *BMJ Open, 9*, e027250. https://doi.org/10.1136/bmjopen-2018-027250

Assari, S. (2017). Social determinants of depression: The intersections of race, gender, and socioeconomic status. *Brain Sciences, 7*(12), 156. https://doi.org/10.3390/brainsci7120156

Bhardwaj, R. N. (2019). *Determinants of mental health: A socioeconomic perspective*. Research Gate. ISBN: 978-1-9991328-0-4.

Kirkbride, J. B., Anglin, D. M., Colman, I., Dykxhoorn, J., Jones, P. B., Patalay, P., Pitman, A., Soneson, E., Steare, T., Wright, T., & Griffiths, S. L. (2024). The social determinants of mental health and disorder: Evidence, prevention, and recommendations. *World Psychiatry, 23*(1), 58–90. https://doi.org/10.1002/wps.21160

Maestre-Miquel, C., López-de-Andrés, A., Ji, Z., de Miguel-Diez, J., Brocate, A., Sanz-Rojo, S., López-Farre, A., Carabantes-Alarcon, D., Jiménez-García, R., & Zamorano-León, J. J. (2021). Gender differences in the prevalence of mental health, psychological distress, and psychotropic medication consumption in Spain: A nationwide population-based study. *International Journal of Environmental Research and Public Health, 18*(12), 6350. https://doi.org/10.3390/ijerph18126350

Shidhaye, R., & Patel, V. (2010). Association of socio-economic, gender, and health factors with common mental disorders in women: A population-based study of 5703 married rural women in India. *International Journal of Epidemiology, 39*(6), 1510–1521. https://doi.org/10.1093/ije/dyq179

Sinha, S., Sharma, S. M., Shrivastava, P., & Bankwar, V. (2023). Prevalence of mental illness among women in an urban slum area of Jaipur: A cross-sectional study. *Journal of Preventive Medicine and Holistic Health, 9*(2), 86–96.

Villatoro, A. P., Mays, V. M., Ponce, N. A., & Aneshensel, C. S. (2017). Perceived need for mental health care: The intersection of race, ethnicity, gender, and socioeconomic status. *Society and Mental Health, 8*(1), 1–24. https://doi.org/10.1177/2156869317718889

# Dancing Away Stress: Embracing Holistic Well-Being

**K. Karthika**

## 1 Introduction

Stress is a pervasive issue that significantly affects physical, mental, and emotional well-being, necessitating its effective management to maintain a healthy lifestyle. According to the American Psychological Association (2021), chronic stress can have far-reaching implications for physical health, including the development of hypertension, cardiovascular disease, and a weakened immune system. These physical manifestations often exacerbate susceptibility to illnesses, highlighting the profound biological toll of prolonged stress.

The impact of stress extends beyond physical health, deeply affecting mental and emotional stability. Persistent stress is a key contributing factor to mental health conditions such as anxiety, depression, and emotional dysregulation (Mayo Clinic, 2022). Additionally, stress disrupts sleep patterns, which can lead to further cognitive impairments, decreased productivity, and challenges in daily functioning. Interpersonal relationships also suffer, as heightened stress levels often lead to irritability, withdrawal, and conflict, collectively reducing the quality of personal and social interactions.

Long-term exposure to stress compounds its detrimental effects, potentially resulting in chronic conditions such as obesity, diabetes, and metabolic syndrome. The World Health Organization (2020) emphasizes the role of stress as a risk factor for these non-communicable diseases, which are among the leading causes of morbidity and mortality worldwide. The physiological mechanisms underlying these conditions often include dysregulated hormonal responses, chronic inflammation, and behavioural changes such as overeating or physical inactivity.

K. Karthika (✉)
Post Graduate Department of Commerce, NSS Hindu College,
Changanacherry, Kottayam, Kerala, India



S. Batra (ed.), *Socioeconomic Factors, Consumer Health, and Broader Well-Being*,
Advances in Mental Health and Addiction, https://doi.org/10.1007/978-3-032-05634-4_4

Given the multifaceted impacts of stress, adopting effective management strategies is crucial for mitigating its adverse effects. Evidence-based approaches such as mindfulness practices, including meditation and breathing exercises, have been shown to reduce stress-related symptoms and promote emotional regulation (American Psychological Association, 2021). Regular physical activity is another essential component, as it improves mood, enhances sleep, and supports overall physical health. Additionally, fostering social connections and seeking professional counselling when needed are integral to stress management.

Fostering social connections through activities such as dance can significantly reduce stress and enhance holistic well-being. Dance provides a unique platform for individuals to engage with others, promoting social interaction and emotional support, which in turn can alleviate feelings of stress and isolation (Koch et al., 2014). Furthermore, the physical benefits of dance, including increased mobility and fitness, coupled with the mental and emotional benefits of creative expression, contribute to a well-rounded sense of well-being (Quiroga Murcia et al., 2010). The combination of social interaction, physical activity, and emotional release through dance can be powerful in reducing stress, making it a meaningful tool for promoting holistic health.

## 2 Methodology

A descriptive, cross-sectional analysis was conducted to examine the relationship between dance and its effects on stress relief and holistic well-being among 66 dancers in Thripunithura Municipality of Ernakulam District. Participants were selected using a purposive sampling technique, focusing on individuals actively engaged in dance as a regular activity. Data collection involved administering a structured questionnaire that assessed participants' stress levels, mental well-being, and perceptions of holistic health, including components such as concentration, emotions, physical fitness, and cultural connection. Statistical tools employed in the analysis included percentage analysis, mean, standard deviation, rank sum, ANOVA, and the Wilcoxon signed-rank test.

The reliability of the scales was assessed using Cronbach's alpha. The holistic well-being scale, consisting of 32 items, demonstrated excellent internal consistency with a Cronbach's alpha of 0.972. In contrast, the awareness of dance forms scale, which included 12 items, showed acceptable reliability with a Cronbach's alpha of 0.817. Both scales exhibited strong internal consistency, with the holistic well-being scale showing particularly high reliability.

In the study data, the majority of variables violated the assumption of normality, as indicated by the significant results ($p < .05$) from the Shapiro-Wilk test. Therefore, non-parametric tests, such as Wilcoxon signed-rank test, were used for further analysis. This methodology enabled the collection of robust data to examine the relationship between dance and its effects on stress relief and holistic well-being.

### *2.1 Independent Variables*

Socio-demographic variables such as age, income, education, marital status and activity status and childhood experience in dance.

### *2.2 Dependent Variables*

Variables capturing holistic well-being (HWB), such as physical fitness, emotions, culture, stress relief, and concentration.

## 3 Results and Discussions

The demographic analysis of the participants shows that the majority (61%) were aged 36–50 years. Regarding monthly income, 50% of the participants fall into the moderate-income category. Most participants (89%) were married. In terms of educational attainment, 46% had completed post-graduation. Additionally, 71% of the participants were regular employees with a fixed salary. These results (refer Table 1) provide a clear overview of the socio-demographic composition of the sample.

Table 2 refers to the ranking of fitness programmes based on their rank sum and it indicates that dancing is the most preferred fitness activity, securing the top rank with the lowest rank sum of 114. Yoga follows as the second most popular option, with a rank sum of 147, reflecting its significance as a holistic fitness approach.

**Table 1** Socio-demographic profile of dancers

| Categories | Highest | Percent |
|---|---|---|
| Age group | 36–50 years | 61 |
| Monthly income | Moderate | 50 |
| Marital Status | Married | 89 |
| Education | Post-Graduation | 46 |
| Activity Status | Regular employee (earning fixed salary) | 71 |

Source: Primary data

**Table 2** Ranking of fitness programmes

| Fitness programmes | Rank sum | Rank |
|---|---|---|
| Dancing | 114 | 1 |
| Gym | 205 | 4 |
| Zumba | 169 | 3 |
| Yoga | 147 | 2 |
| Aerobics | 219 | 5 |

Source: Primary data

**Table 3** Reasons to consider dance as a physical fitness

| Reasons | No. of respondents | Percent |
|---|---|---|
| Enhanced strength and muscle tone | 11 | 17 |
| Improved flexibility | 34 | 51 |
| Increased stamina and endurance | 13 | 20 |
| No noticeable changes | 4 | 6 |
| Weight management | 4 | 6 |
| Total | 66 | 100 |

Source: Primary data

**Table 4** Reasons to consider dance for mental health benefits

| Reasons | No. of respondents | Percent |
|---|---|---|
| Better focus and mental clarity | 2 | 3 |
| Improved mood and happiness | 27 | 41 |
| Increased self-confidence | 11 | 17 |
| Reduced stress and anxiety | 26 | 39 |
| Total | 66 | 100 |

Source: Primary data

Zumba, with a rank sum of 169, is ranked third, highlighting its appeal as a high-energy fitness programme. Gym and Aerobics, with rank sums of 205 and 219, respectively, are ranked fourth and fifth, indicating relatively lower preferences among participants. These rankings suggest that participants favour creative and holistic fitness activities over traditional or high-intensity programmes.

The findings in Table 3 highlight that the majority of respondents (51%) consider improved flexibility as the primary reason for viewing dance as a form of physical fitness. Increased stamina and endurance were identified by 20% of respondents, while enhanced strength and muscle tone was noted by 17%. A smaller proportion of respondents (6%) reported weight management or experiencing no noticeable changes as reasons for considering dance as a fitness activity. These results suggest that participants largely perceive dance as a fitness activity that enhances flexibility, with secondary benefits in stamina, endurance, and muscle tone.

The data in Table 4 reveals that the primary mental health benefit of dance, as identified by respondents, is improved mood and happiness, cited by 41% of participants. Reduced stress and anxiety were the second most commonly reported benefit, noted by 39% of respondents. Additionally, 17% of participants attributed increased self-confidence to dance, while a smaller proportion (3%) recognized better focus and mental clarity as a benefit. These findings underscore the role of dance in promoting emotional well-being, particularly in enhancing mood and alleviating stress, while also contributing to confidence and mental clarity for some individuals.

The results in Table 5 provide insights into the participants' perceptions of holistic well-being across five components. Stress Relief has the highest mean score ($M = 4.33$, $SD = 0.95$), indicating that participants perceive dance as most effective in alleviating stress. Concentration follows with a mean score of 4.09 ($SD = 1.03$), suggesting a strong association between dance and improved mental focus. Culture

**Table 5** Mean scores for components of holistic well-being

| Components | Mean | Standard deviation (SD) |
|---|---|---|
| Physical Fitness | 3.8636 | 1.01059 |
| Emotions | 3.7652 | 1.04755 |
| Culture | 3.8737 | 1.09936 |
| Stress Relief | 4.3333 | .95183 |
| Concentration | 4.0909 | 1.03039 |

Source: Primary data

**Table 6** ANOVA results for the holistic well-being

| Source | Sum of squares | df | Mean square | *F* | *p* value |
|---|---|---|---|---|---|
| Between People | 257.248 | 65 | 3.958 | | |
| Between Items | 13.728 | 4 | 3.432 | 10.265 | .000* |
| Residual | 86.922 | 260 | 0.334 | | |
| Total (Within) | 100.650 | 264 | 0.381 | | |
| Total (Overall) | 357.898 | 329 | 1.088 | | |

Source: Primary data
Grand mean = 3.9854
* indicate statistical significance at $p < .05$

($M = 3.87$, SD = 1.10) and Physical Fitness ($M = 3.86$, SD = 1.01) are also rated highly, reflecting the cultural significance of dance and its role in physical well-being. Emotions has the lowest mean score ($M = 3.77$, SD = 1.05), though still above average, indicating that dance contributes positively to emotional health but to a slightly lesser extent compared to other components. These findings suggest that dance is perceived as a comprehensive activity supporting various aspects of holistic well-being, with stress relief being its most prominent benefit.

H1: There is a significant difference in the mean scores of at least one pair of the five items.

The analysis shown in Table 6 revealed a statistically significant effect of items on the dependent variable, $F(4, 260) = 10.27$, $p < .001$, indicating that at least one component of holistic well-being significantly differs from the others.

H2: There is a significant difference between stress relief and other aspects of health and well-being (concentration, emotional health, physical fitness, and cultural engagement).

Wilcoxon signed-rank test was conducted to examine the differences between stress relief and four aspects of holistic well-being such as concentration, emotional health, physical fitness, and cultural engagement.

Table 7 indicates the Wilcoxon signed-rank test and it revealed significant differences between stress relief and four aspects of health and well-being: concentration ($Z = -3.369$, $p = .001$), emotional health ($Z = -5.176$, $p < .001$), physical fitness ($Z = -4.066$, $p < .001$), and cultural engagement ($Z = -4.437$, $p < .001$). These results indicate that stress relief is distinct from these components, with emotional health showing the largest difference. The findings suggest that interventions aimed

**Table 7** Wilcoxon signed-rank test results for differences between stress relief and HWB components

| Comparison | *Z* | *p* |
|---|---|---|
| Concentration and stress relief | –3.369 | .001* |
| Emotions and stress relief | –5.176 | .000* |
| Physical fitness and stress relief | –4.066 | .000* |
| Culture and stress relief | –4.437 | .000* |

Source: Primary data
* statistical significance at $p < .05$

at improving well-being should address these areas independently while integrating stress relief strategies to achieve a comprehensive approach to holistic well-being.

The test results support the hypothesis that dance significantly reduces stress levels and promotes holistic well-being. Each component (concentration, emotions, physical fitness, and culture) shows a statistically significant relationship with stress relief, highlighting the holistic benefits of dance for mental and emotional health. This provides strong evidence that dance is an effective tool for managing stress and improving well-being.

## 4 Conclusion

This study provides valuable insights into the positive impact of dance on both physical fitness and mental health. The quantitative survey and statistical analyses revealed that dance significantly contributes to enhancing physical well-being, mental resilience, and emotional balance. The results highlight that dance is not only an effective physical activity but also a powerful tool for managing stress, improving concentration, and fostering cultural connections. These findings reinforce the importance of incorporating dance into wellness programmes, offering a holistic approach to overall health and well-being. Future research could explore the long-term effects of dance on mental health and its potential in diverse populations.

## Bibliography

American Dance Therapy Association. (2020). *Dance/movement therapy and mental health*. Retrieved from https://www.adta.org.

American Psychological Association. (2021). *Stress effects on the body*. Retrieved from https://www.apa.org/topics/stress/body.

Catterall, J. S. (2002). The arts and cognitive development. *Educational Researcher, 31*(7), 5–17. https://doi.org/10.3102/0034654303100700005

Hetland, L. (2000). *The arts and human development: Framing a national research agenda for the arts, lifelong learning, and professional development*. American Council for the Arts.

Kiepe, M. S., & Laffan, G. (2019). The role of dance in enhancing mental well-being: A review of recent research. *International Journal of Mental Health and Physical Activity, 17*(3), 201–213. https://doi.org/10.1080/17977422.2019.1624537

Koch, S. C., Morlinghaus, K., & Fuchs, T. (2014). The joy dance: A model for dance and health promotion. *Arts & Health, 6*(1), 10–22. https://doi.org/10.1080/17533015.2013.876045

Martin, S. D., & Green, D. (2006). *Physical fitness and mental well-being: A review of current literature*. New York University Press.

Matarasso, F. (1997). *Use or ornament: The social impact of participation in the arts*. Comedia.

Mayo Clinic. (2022). *Stress symptoms: Effects on your body and behavior*. Retrieved from https://www.mayoclinic.org/stress-symptoms.

National Dance Education Organization. (2015). *Dance for all: Physical and mental well-being through dance education*. NDEO.

Quested, E., & Duda, J. L. (2010). Exploring the relationship between dance participation and physical and mental well-being in a sample of older adults. *Journal of Aging and Physical Activity, 18*(4), 132–145. https://doi.org/10.1123/japa.18.4.132

Quiroga Murcia, M., Kreutz, G., Clift, S., & Bongard, S. (2010). Shall we dance? An exploration of the perceived benefits of dancing on well-being. *Arts & Health, 2*(2), 149–163. https://doi.org/10.1080/17533015.2010.500191

Stuckey, H. L., & Nobel, J. (2010). The connection between art, healing, and public health: A review of the literature. *American Journal of Public Health, 100*(2), 254–263. https://doi.org/10.2105/AJPH.2008.156497

World Health Organization. (2018). *Physical activity and mental health*. WHO Guidelines for Mental Well-Being.

World Health Organization. (2020). *Mental health and stress management*. Retrieved from https://www.who.int.

# "I Am Alone but Not Lonely": Impact of Living Arrangements on the Quality of Life of Older Adults in India

**Teena Wadhera and Samina Bano**

## 1 Introduction

Living arrangements are the most proximate social environments that decide the extent of quality of life of an individual (Alwin et al., 1985). Different living arrangements reflect diverse family relations and distinct social exchange patterns (Kertzer, 1986; Li et al., 2009; Won & Lee, 1999). Living arrangements are of importance in old age, as living arrangements can have a significant effect on physical and mental health problems in old age (Lund et al., 2000; Waite & Hughes, 1999). Moreover, whether an actual living situation matches one's preferred living situation also influences health and psychological well-being of older adults (Sereny, 2011). Therefore, living arrangements are important determinants of individuals' health, well-being, and quality of life in later life. In India, most older adults live in multigenerational living arrangements, which are characterized by living with children (Samanta et al., 2015) or staying with extended families to fulfill their financial, social, and emotional needs. In such scenarios, these older adults are often found to be compromising their independence, are made to feel unwanted, undesirable, and a liability to children, and are often blamed for encroaching on their children's life making them more vulnerable to social disconnectedness and perceived isolation. In the light of these reasons in India, there is growing interest among older adults to live in active adult communities (Tiwari et al., 2012). These active living communities provide housing facilities to older adults that are senior-friendly and support social activities often encompassing independent and assisted living. These communities provide a more independent and active lifestyle to older adults that

T. Wadhera (✉)
Jagan Institute of Management Studies, Sector-5, Rohini, Delhi, India

S. Bano
Department of Psychology, Jamia Millia Islamia, New Delhi, India

 
S. Batra (ed.), *Socioeconomic Factors, Consumer Health, and Broader Well-Being*, Advances in Mental Health and Addiction, https://doi.org/10.1007/978-3-032-05634-4_5

possibly could help them build strong social networks with similar kinds of people, consequently alleviating their perceived isolation, lack of physical and emotional engagement, and improving the quality of life among them.

As the world's population is rapidly ageing, understanding the associations between quality of life and living arrangements in old age is of interest and importance for healthy ageing and welfare policies for the elderly. There is a dearth of studies that have attempted to understand the effects of living in multigenerational and active living communities on the quality of life of older adults in India. This study aims to determine the potential of active adult communities in reducing social isolation and improving quality of life among older adults. Based on the findings, this study advocates for the development of age-friendly communities in India that foster supportive and inclusive environments for older adults, thereby enhancing the quality of life for older adults.

### *1.1 Multigenerational Living Arrangements and Active Adult Communities*

Traditionally, multigenerational households have been the foundation of Indian family life, offering emotional, financial, and caregiving support to older adults. However, this arrangement also presents challenges that can negatively impact their quality of life. Generational conflicts often arise over financial decisions, household routines, and lifestyle choices, leading to stress and tension among family members (Dhillon et al., 2016). Older adults may also experience a lack of privacy and autonomy, which can cause frustration and reduce self-worth. Their dependence on younger family members for daily needs and emotional support may contribute to a diminished sense of independence (Rajan & Balagopal, 2017). Additionally, older adults are sometimes expected to fulfill the needs of other family members, while neglecting their own health and personal care. The pressure to adapt to younger family members' lifestyles can further contribute to dissatisfaction (Kandapan et al., 2023). To address these concerns, active adult communities offer a promising alternative. These communities are specifically designed for older adults seeking an independent, socially engaging, and fulfilling lifestyle. They provide opportunities for meaningful social interaction through group activities, hobby clubs, and cultural events, helping to combat loneliness. On-site healthcare and wellness services support chronic disease management and promote healthier living. Secure environments, emergency response systems, and accessibility-focused infrastructure ensure a safe and worry-free lifestyle. Moreover, services like housekeeping and maintenance allow older adults to enjoy a stress-free retirement. Educational and recreational programs further enhance their sense of purpose and belonging.

# 2 Methods

## 2.1 Design

With the aim of addressing the study's objective, qualitative research design using thematic methodology was utilized to understand how living arrangements affect the quality of life of older adults in India, specifically in the context of multigenerational living arrangement and living in active adult communities. To investigate this, open-ended and semi-structured interviews were conducted with older adults residing in multigenerational living arrangements ($n = 5$) and active adult communities ($n = 5$). Thematic analysis was employed to conduct an in-depth examination and interpretation of the collected data. This method was used to identify, analyze, and report themes within the given dataset.

## 2.2 Participants

Five participants from multigenerational living arrangements were selected from the Delhi region of India. The first participant was a 75-year-old widow living with her son, daughter-in-law, and two grandsons. The second and third participants were a married couple residing on a separate floor within the same building where their children and grandchildren also lived. The wife was 63 years old, and the husband was 65 years old. They were compelled to live with their married daughter and her family unwillingly after the death of their only son. The fourth and fifth participants were a married couple. The husband was 72 years old, and the wife was 69 years old. They were living with their son, daughter-in-law, and one granddaughter.

The participants from the active adult communities were chosen from a senior living community in Bhiwadi, Rajasthan, India. This community offers independent living in senior apartments for individuals aged 55 and older. The criteria for selecting participants from this community required that their demographic profiles be similar to those of participants chosen from the multigenerational community. The first participant from this senior living community was an 82-year-old widow with three married daughters. The second and third participants were a married couple, with the wife aged 72 and the husband aged 76. They had lost their only son. The fourth and fifth participants were also a married couple, with the husband aged 83 and the wife aged 81. They had three married daughters. None of these participants lived with their children or grandchildren; they had relocated from Delhi and chose to live independently in this senior living community.

## 2.3 Procedures

To collect data, informed consent was obtained from all participants, including the management officials of the senior living community in Bhiwadi, Rajasthan. The research purpose and ethical considerations were thoroughly explained to them. Interviews were conducted in the participants' homes according to their preferences. Semi-structured and open-ended questions were used to explore their perceptions of their living arrangements and quality of life. All interviews were digitally recorded and transcribed verbatim. The interviews were conducted in English, as all participants had a strong command of the language due to their education and previous professions.

## 2.4 Data Analysis

Thematic analysis was used to explore older adults' perceptions of multigenerational and active adult communities, focusing on quality of life and well-being. Transcripts were reviewed multiple times for accuracy, and line-by-line coding was conducted. Codes were grouped into themes, which were refined and named following Braun and Clarke's (2006) guidelines. Inadequate themes were excluded. To ensure reliability and validity, the data and themes were cross-checked by three experts, and the triangulation method was used. This process ensured a comprehensive and accurate analysis of the participants' experiences.

## 2.5 Results

The analysis of qualitative data provided a comprehensive and in-depth understanding of the experiences of older adults living in multigenerational living arrangements and active adult communities. Following the thematic analysis approach outlined by Braun and Clarke (2006), key themes and subthemes were identified from the narratives shared by older adults.

The results are organized and presented by first discussing the themes and subthemes related to older adults residing in multigenerational living arrangements, followed by those pertaining to older adults living in senior living communities. Each theme and subtheme is elaborated upon with relevant examples and direct quotes from participants, offering insights into their lived experiences.

### 2.5.1 Quality of Life of Older Adults Living in Multigenerational Living Arrangement

Under this, themes and subthemes highlight the perceptions of loneliness and causes of social disconnectedness that negatively impact the quality of life of older adults living in multigenerational living arrangements.

#### 2.5.1.1 Perceptions of Loneliness

In multigenerational living arrangements older adults experience significant loneliness that impacts their quality of life. Loneliness is a subjective feeling that has been reported by older adults living in multigenerational living arrangements in the following ways:

*Feeling Lonely and Depressed*

Older adults in multigenerational living arrangements commonly experience loneliness, which leads to feelings of sadness. Often, the lack of companionship and social interaction causes them to feel lonely and depressed. This significantly affects their emotional well-being and quality of life. A widow staying in a regular living community said:

> I feel lonely. The family should understand me and look after me. They should not leave me and should spend time with me. When husband was there, it was fine. But as he is no more, children and grandchildren should be there around me.

This was also evident from the following excerpts:

> Children are busy with their own life. They are busy with work and their own children. But now I have learnt to stay alone and spend time watching TV or talking to my full-time domestic help. She talks to me and then I feel better because I have at least somebody to talk to.

Often, the absence of children made them feel very lonely. This was apparent when one of the participants said:

> I often feel lonely when children are not home. I feel isolated as I have nobody to talk to.

Older adults in multigenerational living arrangements often feel lonely and depressed when their children or grandchildren do not have time for them.

*Anxiety and Fear*

Often, stressful situations at home cause older adults to be anxious and fearful. Their emotional state is closely tied to the atmosphere at home and the behavior of their children. Supporting this connection, two of the respondents said:

> In case of any stressful situation at home, I felt anxious and fearful.

> When children are happy, we are happy. When they are happy, their attitude is good to me. But when they are not happy, then they are not concerned.
>
> Now, children's happiness, is our happiness.

As the emotional state of older adults is tied to the behavior of their children, stressful situations at home or bad behavior of children and grandchildren make them anxious and fearful.

*Negative Comparison with Younger Age*

Older adults living in multigenerational living arrangements often compare their current life with their younger days. This leads to a sense of worthlessness in old age. This is evident from the following excerpt:

> Rarely have sound sleep. Face difficulty in sleeping. Awake till 2:30 A.M. Keep thinking about past, present and future.
>
> I often feel lonely as children are not around. I compare my old age with young age. I had friends and family around me in young age. Now, no one is around. So, I have joined a shop to pass time. I come home from work in the afternoon, to have lunch with wife. In the evenings we watch TV programs together. We don't go for outings.

When older adults compare their younger days with older age, this comparison exacerbates feelings of loneliness and sadness amongst them.

*Lack of Optimism and Irritability*

Older adults living in multigenerational living arrangements find themselves emotionally dependent on their children. Consequently, they lack optimism about their lives and often feel irritated with themselves and those around them. This is evident from the following excerpts:

> Do not feel anxious and depressed when grandchildren or relatives are around. But when alone, feel very irritable.
>
> I often get very anxious when children are not at home or come late. There is no reason for happiness. Now it is children's life. Our time is over.

#### 2.5.1.2 Causes of Social Disconnectedness

Social disconnectedness among older adults living in multigenerational communities is a prevalent issue. This arises from a variety of factors that often have a negative impact on their physical and mental health and quality of life. Based on the experiences of the respondents, below are the primary causes of social disconnectedness among older adults living in multigenerational living arrangements:

### *Dependence on Children for Mobility and Social Meetings*

These older adults living in multigenerational living arrangements are dependent on their children for their mobility and social meetings. This is evident from the following excerpts:

> Children do not have time to take us to relatives. We only connect with relatives and friends through the phone.
>
> Children are busy with their own life. They are busy with work and their own children. But now I have learnt to stay alone and spend time watching TV or talking to my full-time domestic help. She talks to me and then I feel better because I have at least somebody to talk to.
>
> TV is on all the time.

Children and grandchildren have busy schedules or other priorities, which restrict the older adults’ ability to participate in social events or meet relatives or friends regularly. Therefore, they have less engagement with their own peer group or community, which shrinks their social circle and meaningful interactions.

### *Limited Social Network in Neighborhood*

Because of lack of peers in the immediate vicinity, the older adults living in multigenerational living arrangements find limited opportunities for socialization with friends of the same age. This is explained by the following excerpt:

> I had few friends of the same age in the neighborhood to socialize and often could not go out to meet them.
>
> No one in the neighborhood. There are no social events organized in the community. So, pray, read religious books when free.

Older adults living in multigenerational living arrangements often find it difficult to socialize because of a lack of friends of the same age in the vicinity.

### *Household and Caregiving Responsibilities*

Older adults living in multigenerational living arrangements often have responsibilities at home, such as looking after grandchildren and managing household chores. This often restricts their ability to socialize. This is evident from the following excerpt:

> Children expected us to stay home and look after grandchildren and household work.

#### 2.5.1.3 Negative Impact on Quality of Life

*Sleep Disturbances*

Older adults living in multigenerational living arrangements have negative thoughts. They keep comparing their present with their past, which contributes to sleep disturbances. Difficulty in sleeping further affects their mental and physical health, leading to a vicious cycle of sleeplessness and worry and poor quality of life.

*Decreased Emotional Well-Being*

Older adults living in multigenerational living arrangements have pervasive feelings of loneliness, depression, anxiety, and fear that significantly decrease their emotional well-being. Their emotional state is fragile and heavily influenced by their surroundings and interactions with family members.

*Irritability and Lack of Social Engagement*

Older adults living in multigenerational living arrangements often lack optimism and become increasingly irritable, which leads them to withdraw from social interactions. Their dependence on their children for happiness prevents them from seeking out other sources of companionship and fulfillment.

*Lack of Emotional Support*

Older adults living in multigenerational living arrangements may have financial support from children, but the lack of emotional support creates a significant void in their lives. This gap between financial and emotional needs contributes to their overall dissatisfaction and sense of neglect in older adults.

### 2.5.2 Quality of Life of Older Adults Living in Active Adult Community

Older adults living in active adult communities were found to have good mental health and quality of life. This was concluded based on the finding that they appeared happy and optimistic about their lives. Being more cheerful, they laughed often. They had less anxiety and sleep problems and reported less physical ailments. This led to less annoyance with self and others and thus they looked forward to another day with hope and positivity. This was gauged based on the following themes and subthemes:

#### 2.5.2.1 Feelings When Alone

*Perception of Being Alone but Not Lonely*

Older adults in active adult communities distinguish between being alone and feeling lonely. They report feeling content and not lonely despite being physically separated from their children and grandchildren. This is evident from the following excerpt:

> After my husband passed away, I shifted to this senior living community. I have no son but three daughter who are married. And living with them is not a comfortable idea. Here, I found lot of people of the same age welcoming. I may be alone but not lonely because neighborhood and my friends here are concerned and connected, and we look after each other. I feel independent and free. I feel, I am the queen of my kingdom.

Living in an active adult community provides older adults with the companionship of peers who are in a similar stage of life. This builds a sense of camaraderie and understanding among them. Their shared experience leads to the formation of supportive friendships and social networks within the community.

*Desire of Independence*

A notable characteristic of older adults living in active adult communities is their minimal dependence on their children, which contrasts sharply with the experiences of those in multigenerational living communities. They value their independence and the freedom it brings. This is evident from the following excerpts:

> I don't like glued with children. I am happily settled.

> Found generation gap with children and grandchildren. Had emotional turmoil before coming to the senior living community. But after coming here, really liked the place. I feel settled, feel like home.

Many older adults expressed a desire to live independently and not be a burden on their children.

*Autonomy*

Older adults living in active adult communities have minimal dependence on their children, which allows them to maintain a sense of independence and control over their lives. This autonomy fosters self-esteem and reduces feelings of being a burden.

> Do not want to stay in control and confinement of children. Forced husband to come to the senior living community. I am not supposed to work as a babysitter or act as a security guard for children.

Here, older adults appreciate the freedom and autonomy that the active adult community offers, allowing them to enjoy their retirement without the stress of familial responsibilities.

*Peer Support and Engagement*

For older adults living in active adult communities, the presence of peers in the same age group provides significant emotional and social support. Daily interactions, shared activities, and common interests create a strong sense of community and belonging. The supporting excerpts are:

> Never felt lonely after coming to the senior living community. Not much alone time. As the same type of people stays here. They wish, greet and meet on a daily basis.

> I have many friends of the same age here. We sit in the garden and chat for long hours. We meet daily and talk a lot. They come to my place too and we sit for long hours together.

Participation in various organized activities and events helps in maintaining an active and fulfilling lifestyle. These activities provide opportunities for learning new skills, pursuing hobbies, and staying mentally and physically engaged.

> The senior living community organize an inter-community competition called as 'Jashan' annually. They also organize month-end parties to celebrate birthdays and anniversaries. I and others perform in the month-end parties and sing songs.

> I participate in activities and never feel alone. Jointly work with the wife for competitions. Developed interest in singing, dancing and gardening after coming to senior living community.

*Having Active Lifestyle*

For older adults living in active adult communities, participation in organized activities and events keeps them physically and mentally active. This active lifestyle helps them maintain cognitive function, physical health, and overall well-being. This is evident from the following shared experiences:

> Holi, Diwali and Women's Day is celebrated. Do not like kitty parties. But like constructive activities. I like these events that are constructive and positive. I participate in photography competition and ramp walk competition. Won 1st prize in both the competitions.

*Opportunities to Pursue Hobbies*

Older adults living in active adult communities not only enjoyed spending time with their spouse but also pursued hobbies like knitting, gardening, writing poems, doing translation work in literature and household work collectively to keep themselves engaged and active. This was evident from the following narrations:

> I participate in activities and never feel alone. Jointly work with wife for competitions. Developed interest in singing, dancing and gardening after coming to senior living community Now have common interest with wife.

> Fond of reading, so go to library and read books and newspaper. I keep myself busy with activities in senior living community. As I am fond of singing, I like participating in singing competitions. I have won many prizes in singing. People compliment me for singing well in this age.

*Positive and Supportive Environment*

The supportive and positive environment of the senior living communities fosters a sense of well-being and happiness. Regular social interactions, celebrations, and shared experiences contribute to a positive outlook on life. This is supported by the following excerpts:

> I am in the company of good people who talk about positive things.

> I spend a lot of time with my 'Bachelor girls' group'. We have regular kitty parties. Go for lunch. We participate in celebrations and competitions together. We perform in cultural programs, go for movie shows and shopping together.

### 2.5.2.2 Reasons of Social Connectedness

The provided text reveals several themes that highlight the social connectedness experienced by older adults living in active adult communities:

*Engagement in Social Activities*

Older adults living in active adult communities participate in various social activities and games, which help them build and maintain friendships. This is evident from the following narrative:

> I help my wife with household activities. Then play carrom with my friends for three hours every day in the recreational club. I take part in the celebration of festivals. We have a group of friends called 'Bachelors'. We keep going on outings together.

*Freedom of Choice*

Older adults living in older adult communities have the autonomy to choose how they spend their time, engaging in activities that interest them. This is based on the following narrative:

> I like making friends. Have 20–25 friends and like talking to them as I am very talkative. I do gardening, reading books. I do translation work of old songs and books. I do a lot of recycling and make useful things.

*Use of Technology for Social Connectivity*

Older adults living in active adult communities stay connected with their family and friends using technology, such as phones, Facebook, WhatsApp, and iPads. The supporting excerpt is:

> I use a phone to keep in touch with my children and friends on a regular basis. Use Facebook or Facetime to keep connected. Do video chatting and share pictures on the iPad.

*Supportive Community Environment*

Older adults living in active adult communities experience the community environment that supports social interaction and reduces the burden of household responsibilities, allowing more time for social engagement.

> I have many friends of the same age here. We sit in the garden and chat for long hours. We meet daily and talk a lot. They come to my place too and we sit for long hours together. I am in the company of good people who talk positive things.

#### 2.5.2.3 Positive Impact on Quality of Life

*Sense of Independence and Control*

The minimal dependence on their children allows these older adults to maintain a sense of independence and control over their lives.

*Active Social Life*

The communal living setting provides ample opportunities for social interaction, reducing feelings of loneliness and promoting mental and emotional health

*Lower Levels of Stress*

The absence of familial conflicts and responsibilities alleviates stress and anxiety, creating a more peaceful and content living environment.

*Enhanced Physical Health, Mental Stimulation, and Cognitive Health*

The distinction between being alone and being lonely, coupled with strong peer support, significantly enhances the emotional well-being of older adults. They feel connected, supported, and less isolated. Participation in organized activities and events keeps older adults physically and mentally active.

*Social Connections and Emotional Well-Being*

Building and maintaining social relationships through community activities and social gatherings reduces feelings of loneliness and isolation, enhancing emotional well-being.

*Sense of Purpose and Achievement*

The engagement in various hobbies, community activities, and social interactions significantly enhances the quality of life for older adults in active adult communities. These activities promote physical and mental health, provide a sense of purpose and achievement, foster social connections, and improve emotional well-being.

*Leadership and Community Involvement*

Taking on leadership roles and organizing events gives older adults a sense of responsibility and purpose, which can be highly fulfilling and improve their quality of life. The following is the supporting excerpt:

> I am called a leader. I organize many events for the temple and conduct other activities. When I am around people, it makes me very happy.

*Recognition and Validation*

Being recognized for their skills and contributions validates their efforts and boosts their self-esteem, leading to a more positive outlook on life.

## 3 Discussion

The purpose of this study was to examine the influence of living arrangements on the quality of life of older adults living in multigenerational living communities and active adult communities. The themes identified in this study highlight a positive and fulfilling emotional landscape for older adults living in active adult communities. Their sense of independence, reduced anxiety, and active social lives contribute to a significantly higher quality of life compared to their counterparts in multigenerational living communities. The themes identified from older adults living in multigenerational living communities highlight a lifestyle characterized by isolation, reliance on passive entertainment, and frustration due to monotonous tasks. Their coping mechanisms, such as spiritual activities, provide some solace but do not fully compensate for the lack of social engagement and meaningful activities. This results in a lower quality of life compared to those in more supportive and engaging environments like senior living communities. Therefore, this research is in line with previous gerontological research that emphasizes the importance of both primary (family, friends, and neighbors) and secondary groups (social clubs and membership groups) to reduce social isolation among older adults (Lubben, 2017). Human beings are social creatures who desire to belong and to be loved. Having a sense of social connection is fundamental for one's physical and mental health (Ristau, 2011). Lack of social connections is detrimental to health and longevity (Umberson & Karas Montez, 2010). However, strong social connections increase the chance of longevity, improve the immune system, and help people to recover from their diseases faster. When people feel connected, they have less instances of anxiety and depression (Seppala, 2014). Social isolation is seen as "a potent killer" (Lubben, 2017) and thus requires investment in resources and designing of interventions by researchers, practitioners, and policymakers that could act as a buffer against its dire consequences. It is also imperative for the family and the society to collectively provide social support to older adults so that they could experience healthy ageing by getting the physical and emotional support that is necessary for developing and maintaining the sense of belongingness among them.

## 4 Implications

The practical implications of comprehending the effects of living arrangements on the quality of life of older adults are significant across various realms. Since older adults are at a steeper risk for loneliness, depression, and cognitive decline, the healthcare providers can offer mental health interventions, such as counselling, social support programs, to combat isolation. In multigenerational living arrangements, community efforts can be directed toward encouraging participation of older adults in community programs or fostering intergenerational activities where younger people engage with the elderly. Families can be counselled for understanding the need and means to provide emotional and social support to older adults living with them. The understanding that living arrangements can have a direct bearing on their quality of life can encourage the development of more affordable and accessible assisted living options. Moreover, by acknowledging the different needs of older adults based on their living arrangements, policymakers can create laws that promote better care for older adults, such as incentives for families providing care or by providing access to economical active senior living communities or retirement homes.

The social implications of understanding the role of living arrangements on the quality of life of older adults have a significant impact on shaping societal attitudes and support systems for older adults. These implications affect the social framework, relationships within families and communities at large. Families can be encouraged to stay connected with older relatives to make them feel included and valued. Various community-based initiatives such as senior centers, volunteer programs, or neighborhood watch programs can assist in combating isolation by building opportunities for older adults to interact with their peers and participate with them in social activities. Thus, improving the quality of life for older adults requires a holistic approach that addresses these various factors that promotes sportive and inclusive environment for ageing.

## 5 Conclusion

The process of ageing cannot be halted. Perhaps, the process of ageing could be made a fulfilling experience by giving an environment to older adults that includes care and attention. Understanding and productive engagement could help in alleviating loneliness and isolation among older adults through which their mental health could be improved. This study emphasizes that senior living community provides such environment that improves mental well-being among older adults. However, it is not feasible for many older adults to shift to senior living communities because of social, financial, psychological, and physical difficulties. Therefore, it becomes the collective responsibility of children, grandchildren, relatives, neighborhood, and resident welfare associations to not discard older adults but take active actions to promote the concept of healthy ageing among them. This can be done by actively engaging older adults in productive and constructive activities that reduce their loneliness and make them build strong social networks that will go a long way in improving their mental health.

## References


Alwin, D. F., Converse, P. E., & Martin, S. S. (1985). Living arrangements and social integration. *Journal of Marriage and the Family, 47*, 319–334.

Braun, V., & Clarke, V. (2006). Using thematic analysis in psychology. *Qualitative Research in Psychology, 3*(2), 77–101.

Dhillon, P., Ladusingh, L., & Agrawal, G. (2016). Ageing and changing patterns in familial structure for older persons in India: a decomposition analysis. *Quality in Ageing and Older Adults, 17*(2), 83–96.

Kandapan, B., Pradhan, J., & Pradhan, I. (2023). Living arrangement of Indian elderly: a predominant predictor of their level of life satisfaction. *BMC Geriatrics, 23*(1), 88.

Kertzer, D. I. (1986). A life course approach to coresidence. *Current Perspectives on Aging and the Life Cycle, 2*, 1–22.

Li, L. W., Zhang, J., & Liang, J. (2009). Health among the oldest-old in China: which living arrangements make a difference? *Social Science & Medicine, 68*(2), 220–227.

Lubben, J. (2017). Addressing social isolation as a potent killer! *Public Policy & Aging Report, 27*(4), 136–138.

Lund, R., Modvig, J., Due, P., & Evald Holstein, B. (2000). Stability and change in structural social relations as predictor of mortality among elderly women and men. *European Journal of Epidemiology, 16*, 1087–1097.

Rajan, S. I., & Balagopal, G. (2017). Caring India: an introduction. In *Elderly care in India: Societal and state responses* (pp. 1–36). Springer.

Ristau, S. (2011). People do need people: Social interaction boosts brain health in older age. *Generations, 35*(2), 70–76.

Samanta, T., Chen, F., & Vanneman, R. (2015). Living arrangements and health of older adults in India. *Journals of Gerontology Series B: Psychological Sciences and Social Sciences, 70*(6), 937–947.

Seppala, E. (2014). *Connectedness & health: The science of social connection*. Stanford Medicine The Center for Compassion and Altruism Research and Education. Retrieved December 1, 2024, from http://ccare.stanford.edu/uncategorized/connectedness-health-the-science-of-social-connectioninfographic/.

Sereny, M. (2011). Living arrangements of older adults in China: The interplay among preferences, realities, and health. *Research on Aging, 33*(2), 172–204.

Tiwari, S. C., Pandey, N. M., & Singh, I. (2012). Mental health problems among inhabitants of old age homes: A preliminary study. *Indian Journal of Psychiatry, 54*(2), 144–148.

Umberson, D., & Karas Montez, J. (2010). Social relationships and health: A flashpoint for health policy. *Journal of Health and Social Behavior, 51*(1_suppl), S54–S66.

Waite, L. J., & Hughes, M. E. (1999). At risk on the cusp of old age: Living arrangements and functional status among black, white and Hispanic adults. *The Journals of Gerontology Series B: Psychological Sciences and Social Sciences, 54*(3), S136–S144.

Won, Y.-H., & Lee, G. R. (1999). Living arrangements of older parents in Korea. *Journal of Comparative Family Studies, 30*(2), 315–328.

# Index




S. Batra (ed.), *Socioeconomic Factors, Consumer Health, and Broader Well-Being*, Advances in Mental Health and Addiction,
https://doi.org/10.1007/978-3-032-05634-4

Made in the USA
Monee, IL
14 September 2026

62974050R00046